日本語の森

教えて！
ゆか先生

日本語会話表現60

村上 由佳 著

はじめに

本書を手に取っていただき、本当にありがとうございます。

この本は、私が日本語教師になってから今まで、学生のみんなからもらった、たくさんのメッセージやコメントをもとにして作ったものです。

本を書きながら、みんなへの"ありがとう"という気持ちをたくさん思い出しました。

「日本語」を通して、みなさまと出会えたことをとてもうれしく思っています。

最後まで楽しんで読んでもらえるとうれしいです。

日本語の森
村上 由佳

目次 Table of Contents

はじめに ……………………………………………………………………… 003

ゆか先生の自己紹介 & 日本語の森の紹介 ………………………………… 008

本書の構成 & 使い方 ……………………………………………………… 012

第1章 もしかして使っちゃってる？ 不自然 & 失礼な表現 …………… 016

《 フレーズ編 》

● **はじめまして** ……………………………………………………………… 017

どうぞ、よろしく ｜ 名前は何ですか？ ｜ はじめまして。私は村上です
あなたは何人ですか？ ｜ 何歳ですか？

mini COLUMN 日本人のあいさつ ……………………………… 028

● **あいさつ & 断り方** ……………………………………………………… 029

ゆかちゃん、こんにちは！ ｜ （会社で）こんにちは / こんばんは
さようなら ｜ どういたしまして ｜ すみません、ちょっと… ｜ 結構です

mini COLUMN 日本人のラーメンの食べ方 ……………………… 042

● **日常会話** …………………………………………………………………… 043

今ひまですか？ ｜ お菓子がほしいですか？ ｜ 上手ですね
先生にお菓子を買ってあげます ｜ あー、はいはい ｜ 愛しています

《 **会話編** 》

ゆか先生とあやの先生の出会い ｜ 仕事のあとは、かんぱい！

北海道出身のあやの先生

> mini COLUMN　日本人が漢字を勉強する方法 ・・・・・・・・・・・・・・・・・・・・・ 062

第2章　これってどういうこと？ 意味がややこしい言葉 ・・・・・・・・ 064

《 **フレーズ編** 》

● **意味がいっぱいある言葉** ・・・・・・・・・・・・・・・・・・・・・・・・・・・・・・・・・・・・・ 065

大丈夫 ｜ いいです ｜ すみません

> mini COLUMN　日本の電車 ・・・・・・・・・・・・・・・・・・・・・・・・・・・・・・・・・・・・・・ 078

● **教科書と意味が違う言葉** ・・・・・・・・・・・・・・・・・・・・・・・・・・・・・・・・・・ 079

全然 ｜ まあまあ ｜ おかげで

> mini COLUMN　日本の給食 ・・・・・・・・・・・・・・・・・・・・・・・・・・・・・・・・・・・・・ 086

● **違いがややこしい言葉** ・・・・・・・・・・・・・・・・・・・・・・・・・・・・・・・・・・・・・ 087

する予定 & するつもり ｜ 〜でいいです & 〜がいいです

こういう & そういう & ああいう

● **意味がややこしい言い方** ・・・・・・・・・・・・・・・・・・・・・・・・・・・・・・・・・・ 095

「明日まで」って、いつまで？｜「前のページ」って、先？後ろ？

「1日おきに来る」って、いつ来るの？

「もらってあげてくれる？」って、だれに何をするの？

《 会話編 》

日本語の森でお仕事中 ｜ 結婚したい？ ｜ 仕事の相談

mini COLUMN　日本の学校のルール ································· 110

第3章　これができたら、会話上級者！ ··················· 112

《 フレーズ編 》

● **便利なあいづち** ··· 113

なるほど ｜ いいね ｜ そうなの？ ｜ うーん ｜ へぇー

mini COLUMN　便利なあいづち「さしすせそ」················ 124

● **にごす言葉** ··· 125

なんか ｜ 〜っていうか ｜ 〜みたいな ｜ まあ ｜ 〜ないこと ｜ ない

〜とか ｜ 〜けど ｜ 〜かな

mini COLUMN　「にごす言葉」について ····························· 134

● **クッション言葉** ··· 135

もしよかったら… ｜ 悪いんだけど… ｜ せっかくなんだけど…

個人的には… ｜ 知ってるかもしれないけど…

信じられないかもしれないけど… ｜ 〜したんだけど…

mini COLUMN　「クッション言葉」について ······················ 150

- **怒るときの言葉** ……………………………………………… 152
  なんで？ ｜ むかつく ｜ ふざけないで ｜ ありえない！
  いらいらする ｜ バカにしてる？ ｜ もういい！

    mini COLUMN　日本人が怒るとき ……………………………………… 160

- **気持ちを伝える言葉** ………………………………………… 161
  疲れたー！ ｜ つらい ｜ おいしい！

《 **会話編** 》

　みんなでお昼ごはんを食べに行こう ｜ ゆか先生はラーメンが大好き！
　ごちそうさま！でも…

    mini COLUMN　あいづちの役割 …………………………………………… 174
    mini COLUMN　便利な形容詞「やばい」 ………………………………… 176

ゆか先生のおすすめ勉強法 ……………………………………… 178
おすすめのYouTube番組 ………………………………………… 182
あとがき …………………………………………………………… 184

ゆか先生の自己紹介 Yuka-Sensei's Self-Introduction

はじめまして。村上由佳です。

1992年3月30日生まれ、出身は日本の兵庫県です。日本人です。

私の仕事は日本語教師です。みんなから「ゆか先生」と呼ばれています。

「日本語の森」で日本語の授業をしたり、動画を作ったりしています。

好きな食べ物はラーメン、好きなお菓子は「じゃがりこ」と「つぶグミ」、

好きなお酒はビールと日本酒です。

いつかみんなと乾杯して朝までお酒を飲むのが夢！ みなさん、どうぞよろしくお願いします。

Nice to meet you, I'm Yuka Murakami.
I was born on March 30, 1992 in Hyogo Prefecture, Japan. I'm Japanese.
I work as a Japanese teacher. Everyone calls me "Yuka-sensei."
I teach Japanese classes and make videos at 'Nihongo no Mori.'
My favorite food is ramen, my favorite snacks are "じゃがりこ (potato sticks)" and "つぶグミ (fruit gummies,)" and my favorite alcohols are beer and Japanese sake.
My dream is to someday have a toast with everyone and drink until the morning! I'm looking forward to studying with you more in the months and years ahead.

村上由佳先生

もりおくん

ゆか先生の自己紹介

私は大学を卒業してから、いろんな仕事をしてきました。日本語教師になったのは26歳のときで、ベトナムで日本語教師として働き始めました。それまでは日本で留学生のサポートをする仕事をしていました。そのときに、仕事熱心でいつも人のことを思いやるベトナム人と出会い、ベトナムに興味を持ったんです。同時に、彼らが通っている日本語学校というものの存在を知りました。「日本語の先生って面白そう！」と思って、日本語教師になるための学校に通ったんです。気付いたら会社を辞めて、ベトナムへ飛び立っていました。

I've done a lot of different jobs since graduating from university. I was 26 when I became a Japanese teacher and I started working as a Japanese teacher in Vietnam. Up until then, I had been working at a job in Japan supporting study abroad students. It was then that I encountered how enthusiastic about their work and caring Vietnamese people always are, and I became interested in the country. At that same time, I found out about the Japanese language schools they attend. I thought teaching Japanese seemed really interesting, so I went to school to become a teacher. The next thing I knew, I had quit my job and was heading to Vietnam.

これまで何度か海外で生活しましたが、毎日が本当に楽しかったんです。それは、「ご飯食べた？」「何か困ったことはない？」といつも私を気にかけてくれる現地の方々のおかげだったと思います。だから私も、日本語を教えるという仕事を通して恩返しできたらいいなと思っています。日本語を外国語として見ることはすごく面白いし、どうやってわかりやすく教えようか考えることも本当に楽しいです。そして、世界中の人たちから「ありがとう」と言ってもらえることが、何よりも幸せです。私にとって、日本語教師はまさに「天職」です。

I've lived abroad on several occasions, and I really enjoyed each and every day. I think it was thanks to the local people who always looked out for me, asking "Have you eaten?" or "Are you having any difficulties?" I hope to be able to give back through my work as a Japanese teacher. Seeing Japanese as a foreign language is so interesting, and it's really fun to think up ways of teaching it that are easy to understand. And above all, it makes me happy to to hear "Thank you" from people all over the world. For me, being a Japanese language teacher is truly my vocation.

日本語の森の紹介 Introducing 'Nihongo no Mori'

「日本語の森」って？
What is 'Nihongo no Mori'?

「日本語の森」は日本にある会社です。YouTubeのチャンネルで、日本語をわかりやすく面白く学べる動画をたくさん配信しています。私はもともとベトナムの日本語センターで授業をしながら、日本語が楽しく学べる動画を作っていました。そして1年が過ぎたころ、次は全世界の学習者向けに「日本語の森」で動画を配信するようになったんです。「ゆか先生はどうしてベトナムに住んでいるんですか？」とよく聞かれるのですが、最初はベトナム人の学習者向けに日本語を教えていて、そのあと「日本語の森」で仕事をするようになったからなんです。「日本語の森」では、できるだけ簡単な日本語を使って日本語を教えています。だから、基本的な日本語がわかる人は、だれでも「日本語の森」で勉強することができるんですよ。

'Nihongo no Mori' is a company in Japan. We put out a lot of easy-to-understand and interesting videos on our YouTube channel. I had originally been making videos to make learning Japanese fun while teaching at a Japanese language center in Vietnam. Then, a year later, I started making videos for learners all over the world through 'Nihongo no Mori.' I'm often asked why I live in Vietnam, and it's because I had been teaching Japanese to Vietnamese learners at first before working in 'Nihongo no Mori.' 'Nihongo no Mori' teaches Japanese using the simplest Japanese possible. That's why anyone who can understand basic Japanese can study at 'Nihongo no Mori.'

日本語を楽しく学ぼう！

「日本語の森」のこれまでとこれから

The past and future of 'Nihongo no Mori'

「日本語の森」YouTube チャンネルがスタートしたのは 2013 年です。今では「日本語の森のゆか先生」と言ってもらえることも多くなったんですが、私が「日本語の森」の仲間になったのは 2019 年です。「ベトナムで日本語を教えよう」と思っていただけだった私が、まさかオンラインで、しかも全世界に向けて授業をすることになるなんて全く想像もしていませんでした。そして本を書くことになるなんて…何が起きるかわからないですね！

そして 2020 年には、ネット講義サイト「日本語の森」をオープンしました。これからも「日本語の森」の仲間を増やしながら、もっともっとわかりやすくて面白い授業を世界中に届けていきたいと思っています。

The 'Nihongo no Mori' YouTube channel began in 2013. Nowadays, many people call me "Yuka-sensei from 'Nihongo no Mori,'" but I only joined 'Nihongo no Mori' in 2019. I just thought I'd teach Japanese in Vietnam, and I never imagined that I would end up teaching Japanese online and to learners all over the world. Now I'm writing a book…you never know what will happen!
And in 2020, we launched the 'Nihongo no Mori' online course site. Going forward, I'd like to continue increasing the number of 'Nihongo no Mori' pals and provide even more easy-to-understand and interesting lessons for the whole world.

本書の構成 & 使い方 Structure of This Book & How to Use

フレーズ編（第1章・2章）

- **勉強するフレーズ**
  Phrases to be learned

- **勉強するフレーズを使った会話**
  Conversations using the phrases to be learned

- **英語翻訳**
  English translation

- **フレーズの説明**
  もりおくんの質問に、ゆか先生が答えます。
  Yuka-sensei will respond to Morio-kun's explanation.

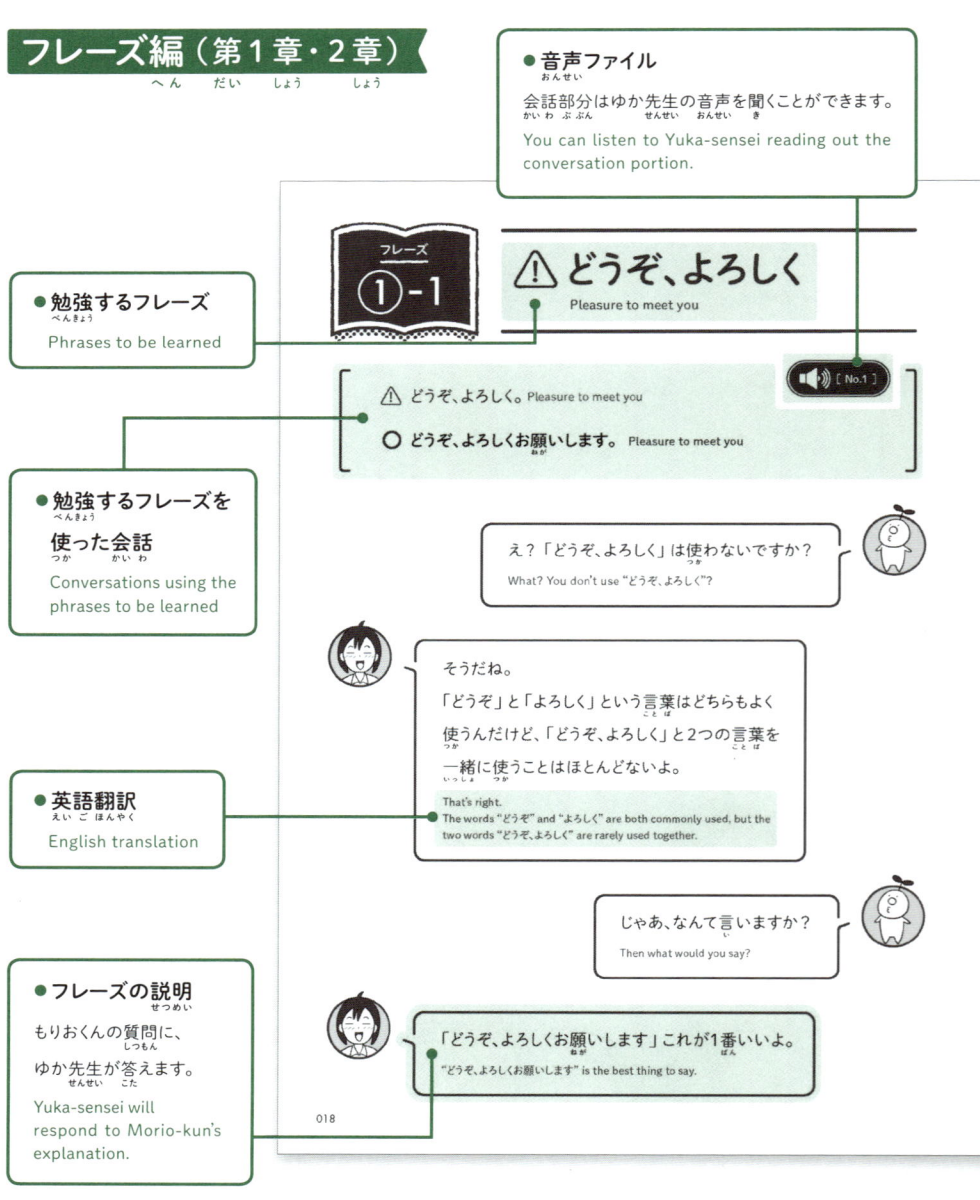

- **音声ファイル**
  会話部分はゆか先生の音声を聞くことができます。
  You can listen to Yuka-sensei reading out the conversation portion.

フレーズ ①-1

⚠ どうぞ、よろしく
Pleasure to meet you

[No.1]

⚠ どうぞ、よろしく。Pleasure to meet you

○ どうぞ、よろしくお願いします。Pleasure to meet you

え？「どうぞ、よろしく」は使わないですか？
What? You don't use "どうぞ、よろしく"?

そうだね。
「どうぞ」と「よろしく」という言葉はどちらもよく使うんだけど、「どうぞ、よろしく」と2つの言葉を一緒に使うことはほとんどないよ。

That's right.
The words "どうぞ" and "よろしく" are both commonly used, but the two words "どうぞ、よろしく" are rarely used together.

じゃあ、なんて言いますか？
Then what would you say?

「どうぞ、よろしくお願いします」これが1番いいよ。
"どうぞ、よろしくお願いします" is the best thing to say.

音声ダウンロードはここから
You can download the audio from here.

https://ask-books.com/book-details/?slug=9784866394534#audio-play

はじめまして｜Nice to meet you

「どうぞ、よろしく」って言ったら、相手はどう思いますか？
What would the other person think if you were to say "どうぞ、よろしく"?

もし初対面で「どうぞ、よろしく」って言われたら、「なんだこいつ、偉そうだな」って思うかな。
自己紹介をするのは、初めて会った人と話すときだよ。だから、できるだけ丁寧に話した方が印象はよくなる。
If you say "どうぞ、よろしく" when meeting someone for the first time, they'd think "Who's this guy, so high and mighty?" You introduce yourself when talking to someone you've met for the first time, right? So you'll give off a better impression if you speak as politely as possible.

● 登場人物　Characters

ゆか先生　あやの先生　もりおくん

なるほど！
I see!

● まとめ　Summary
このページで勉強したことの中で大切なことを、わかりやすくまとめています。

Summarizes the important things you have learned on the page in an easy-to-understand manner.

まとめ　初めて会う人に「どうぞ、よろしく」は失礼！
It's rude to say "どうぞ、よろしく" to someone you've met for the first time!

丁寧な言い方　……… どうぞ、よろしくお願いします。
Polite phrasing
※友だちや年が近い人には「よろしく！」と言うこともあるよ！
※Sometimes people will say "よろしく！" to friends and people who are close in age!

たまには休んでね

フレーズ編（第3章）

なるほど A

B 例文 Example sentence

「私のお母さん、チョコレートが大好きだったから、私も好きになったんだ。」
「なるほどね。」
"My mom loved chocolate, so I came to love it too."
"I see."

D 意味 Meaning
- 相手が言った言葉に対して、「よくわかった」「その通りだ」という気持ちを表すときに使う
- 相手が言って初めて気がついたことがあるときによく使う
- It's used to express the feeling that what the other person's said is "well understood" or "that's right."
- You often use it for something you've realised for the first time since the other person said it.

E 使い方 Usage
[1] 「今日、頭が痛くてさ。」
「なるほど、だから朝からあんまりしゃべってなかったんだ。」
"I've got a headache today."
"I see, that's why you haven't talked much since this morning."

[2] 「『日本語の森』の人気があるのは、いい先生がたくさんいるからなんだって。」
「なるほど！」
"I heard the reason why 'Nihongo no Mori' is so popular is because they have a lot of good teachers."
"I see!"

F ポイント Point
「なるほど」という言葉は、「あなたの言っていることは正しい」というように、相手の言ったことを評価している印象を与えることがあります。先生や上司に使うと失礼になる場合がありますよ。使うときは「なるほど！そうなんですね！」や「あぁー！なるほど！知らなかったです！」のように気持ちを込めて言った方がいいです。

The word "なるほど" can give the impression that you're evaluating what the other person's said, like "what you're saying is right." It can be rude if you use it with teachers or bosses. You should say it with feeling when using it, like "なるほど！そうなんですね！" or "あぁ〜！なるほど！I didn't know that!"

G 似ているフレーズ Similar Phrases

● 確かに！ Certainly！
相手の意見に対して「私もそう思う」と強く同意する気持ちを表す。
Expresses strong agreement with the other person's opinion, like "I think so too!"

● そうですね That's so
相手の意見に対して、同意する気持ちを表す。軽い同意のときにも使える１番使いやすい方。
Expresses agreement with the other person's opinion. It's easiest phrase to use that can also be used to express light agreement.

● おっしゃる通りです You are correct
「あなたの言っていることに同意します」という意味。「おっしゃる」は「言う」の尊敬語なので、先生や会社の上司によく使う言い方。
Means "I agree with what you are saying." "おっしゃる" is the respectful form of "言う," so it's often used towards teachers and bosses.

「なるほど！確かにそうですね！
おっしゃる通りです。」のように、
一緒に使うこともありますよ。
Sometimes they're also used together,
as in 「なるほど！確かにそうですね！
おっしゃる通りです。」

A 勉強するフレーズ
Phrases to be learned

B 勉強するフレーズを使った会話
Conversations using the phrases to be learned

C 音声ファイル
会話部分はゆか先生の音声を聞くことができます。
You can listen to Yuka-sensei reading out the conversation portion.

D 意味
意味を確認しましょう。フレーズによっては、いろんな意味がある場合があります。
Check the meaning. Depending on the phrase, there may be various different meanings.

E 使い方
会話の中でどのように使われるのか確認しましょう。
Check how it's used in conversation.

F ポイント
勉強したフレーズを使うときのポイントを説明しています。
Explains the key points when using the phrases you've studied.

G 似ているフレーズ
意味が似ていて、同じような場面で使えるフレーズを紹介しています。
Introduces phrases that have similar meanings and can be used in similar situations.

会話編
かいわへん

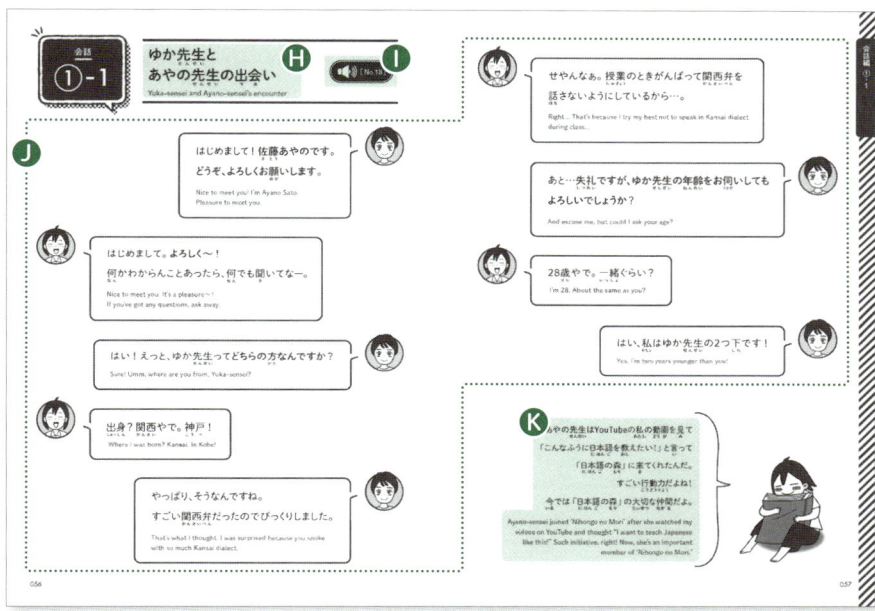

H 会話のタイトル
かいわ

Conversation title

I 音声ファイル
おんせい

会話部分はゆか先生とあやの先生の音声を聞くことができます。
かいわ ぶ ぶん せんせい せんせい おんせい き

You can listen to Yuka-sensei reading out the conversation portion.

J 会話
かいわ

ゆか先生とあやの先生の会話です。
せんせい せんせい かいわ

Conversations between Yuka-sensei and Ayano-sensei.

K ゆか先生のつぶやき
せんせい

会話に関係のあることについてゆか先生がつぶやいています。
かいわ かんけい せんせい

Yuka-sensei comments about things related to the conversation.

もしかして使っちゃってる？
不自然 & 失礼な表現

Could you be using these?
Unnatural & rude expressions

- P.17〜 　はじめまして
  Nice to meet you

- P.29〜 　あいさつ & 断り方
  Greetings & How to say 'no'

- P.43〜 　日常会話
  Daily conversation

1章、はじまるよ！

はじめまして

― Nice to meet you ―

どうぞ、よろしく
Pleasure to meet you

 [No.1]

⚠ どうぞ、よろしく。 Pleasure to meet you

○ どうぞ、よろしくお願いします。 Pleasure to meet you

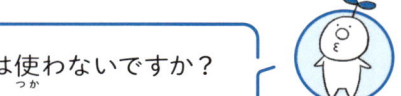

え?「どうぞ、よろしく」は使わないですか?
What? You don't use "どうぞ、よろしく"?

そうだね。
「どうぞ」と「よろしく」という言葉はどちらもよく使うんだけど、「どうぞ、よろしく」と2つの言葉を一緒に使うことはほとんどないよ。

That's right.
The words "どうぞ" and "よろしく" are both commonly used, but the two words "どうぞ、よろしく" are rarely used together.

じゃあ、なんて言いますか?
Then what would you say?

「どうぞ、よろしくお願いします」これが1番いいよ。
"どうぞ、よろしくお願いします" is the best thing to say.

はじめまして | Nice to meet you

> 「どうぞ、よろしく」って言ったら、
> 相手はどう思いますか？
>
> What would the other person think if you were to say "どうぞ、よろしく"?

> もし初対面で「どうぞ、よろしく」って言われたら、
> 「なんだこいつ、偉そうだな」って思うかな。
> 自己紹介をするのは、初めて会った人と話すときだよね？
> だから、できるだけ丁寧に話した方が印象はよくなるよ。
>
> If you say "どうぞ、よろしく" when meeting someone for the first time, I feel they'd think "Who's this guy, so high and mighty?" You introduce yourself when talking to someone you've met for the first time, right? So you'll give off a better impression if you speak as politely as possible.

> なるほど！
>
> I see!

まとめ 初めて会う人に「どうぞ、よろしく」は失礼！

It's rude to say "どうぞ、よろしく" to someone you've met for the first time!

丁寧な言い方 ……… どうぞ、よろしくお願いします。

Polite phrasing

※友だちや年が近い人には「よろしく！」と言うこともあるよ。

※Sometimes people will say "よろしく！" to friends and people who are close in age!

名前は何ですか？
What's your name?

⚠️ 名前は何ですか？　What's your name?

○ お名前をお伺いしてもよろしいでしょうか。　May I ask your name?

実は、日本人同士の会話で「名前は何ですか？」と聞くことはほとんどないよ。

"名前は何ですか？" is actually rarely heard in conversations among Japanese people.

そうですか。
じゃあ、「お名前は…？」という聞き方はよく使いますか？

Is that so? Then, do you phrase it "お名前は…?" often?

うん！この聞き方をするときは、「お名前は！？」と勢いよく聞くよりも「お名前は…？」と少し申し訳なさそうな顔をするともっといいよ。

Yeah! When phrasing it like this, it's better to make a slightly apologetic face while asking "お名前は…?" rather than asking energetically, like "お名前は！?"

「お名前をお伺いしてもよろしいでしょうか」と聞いて、断られることはありますか？

Are there times people might refuse when you ask "お名前をお伺いしてもよろしいでしょうか?"

はじめまして ｜ Nice to meet you

ないと思う！私は断られたことないよ。
I don't think so! I've never had someone refuse.

じゃあ、何でわざわざ
「お伺いしてもよろしいでしょうか」と聞くんですか？
Then why do you bother to say "お伺いしてもよろしいでしょうか?"

相手が断らないとわかっていてもわざわざ
「お伺いしてもよろしいでしょうか」と聞く。
これが丁寧な日本語なんだよね。
Even if you know the other person won't refuse, we still take the trouble to say, "お伺いしてもよろしいでしょうか?" This is what polite Japanese is like.

むずかしいな〜。
So difficult...

まとめ 「名前は何ですか？」は失礼！
"名前は何ですか?" is rude!

おすすめの言い方 Recommended phrasing

[1]「お名前をお伺いしてもよろしいでしょうか」

[2]「お名前は…？」＋ 少し申し訳なさそうな声と表情
"お名前は…?" + A slightly apologetic tone and expression

⚠️ はじめまして。私は村上です。

Nice to meet you. As for me, I'm Murakami.

⚠️ はじめまして。私は村上です。
Nice to meet you. As for me, I'm Murakami.

○ はじめまして。村上です。
Nice to meet you. I'm Murakami.

え！これはどこが変なんですか？
Huh! What's wrong with this one?

自分の名前を言うときに「私は…」と言うことはほとんどないよ。
だって、私のことを話しているんだから、私の名前以外ありえないでしょ？

When you say my name, it's rare to say "私は…" Besides, you're talking about yourself, so it couldn't be anyone's name but yours, right?

知らなかったです。
「私は…」を言うと少し不自然なんですね。
でも、「私は…」を使うこともありますよね？

I didn't know that.
So it's a bit unnatural to say "私は…" But sometimes you say "私は," right?

はじめまして | Nice to meet you

うん、強調して言いたいときに使うよ。
例えば、他の人を紹介していて
「Mさんは学生です。Yさんも学生です。私は教師です。」
こういうときは、「私は…」って言った方がいいよ。

Yeah, you use it to emphasize what you want to say.
For example, when you're introducing someone, you'd say, "M-san is a student. Y-san is also a student. As for me, I'm a teacher." In these kind of situations, it's better to use "私は…"

なるほど。
自己紹介で最初に言うときは「私は…」は
言わない方がいいということですね。

I see.
So when first introducing yourself, you shouldn't say "私は…"

そういうこと！

That's right!

まとめ

自己紹介のときは、「私は…」を言わない方が自然！

When introducing yourself, it's more natural not to say "私は…"!

あなたは何人ですか？
What nationality are you?

> ⚠ あなたは何人ですか？　What nationality are you?
>
> ○ どちらの方ですか？　Where are you from?

 [No.4]

えー！ これはよく使っていました！
Huh! I've used this a lot!

この言葉がすごく失礼というわけではないよ。
ただ、違う言い方をした方が印象がいいよ。「何人ですか？」と聞くと「私は〜人だけど、あなたは別の国の人なんでしょ？」という感じに聞こえる場合があるかな。

It's not that this phrase is super rude.
However, phrasing it differently gives a better impression.
When you ask "何人ですか?" I think it may sound like you're saying "I'm from 〜, but you're from another country, right?"

何と聞くのが丁寧ですか？
What would be a polite way to ask?

「どちらの方ですか？」とか「お国はどちらですか？」と聞くと、もっと丁寧な印象になるよ。

Asking "どちらの方ですか？(Where you from?)" or "お国はどちらですか？(Which country are you from?)" gives a more polite impression.

はじめまして | Nice to meet you

なるほど。
I see.

「どちらの方ですか」という聞き方は、日本人同士で出身地を聞きたいときにも使えるよ。「ご出身はどちらですか」もよく使うね。

The question "どちらの方ですか?" can also be used when Japanese people want to ask each other's hometowns.
"ご出身はどちらですか?(Where were you born)?" is also used often.

ちなみに、ゆか先生はどちらの方ですか?
By the way, where are you from, Yuka-sensei?

神戸やで〜!
Kobe yade〜!

※「やで」は神戸の方言。「神戸です」の意味
※ "やで" is from Kobe dialect. Means "I'm from Kobe."

まとめ

「あなたは何人ですか?」は、もっと丁寧な言い方がある!

There's a nicer way to ask "あなたは何人ですか?"!

おすすめの言い方 ……… 「どちらの方ですか?」「お国はどちらですか?」
Recommended phrasing

※言葉自体が失礼なわけではないので、気にしすぎる必要はない
※The phrase itself is not rude, so there's no need to worry too much.

何歳ですか？
How old are you?

⚠️ 何歳ですか？
How old are you?

○ 失礼ですが、年齢をお伺いしてもよろしいでしょうか？
Excuse me, but could I ask your age?

[No.5]

これは、「名前は何ですか？」と少し似ていますね。
This is a bit like "名前は何ですか？"

そう！名前も年齢も相手にとって大切な情報なので、聞くときは丁寧であればあるほどいいね。
Yes! Both the other person's name and age are important information to them, so the more polite you are when asking, the better.

「失礼ですが…」は必要ですか？
Do you need to say "失礼ですが...(Excuse me...)"?

年齢を聞くときは、あったほうがいいね。
名前を聞くときも「失礼ですが」をつけるともっといいかな！
でも、特に年齢は聞くと「失礼」になってしまうことが多いから、つけた方がいいと思うよ。

When asking someone's age, you should say it. It's more polite to say "失礼ですが" when asking for someone's name too! But I think it's better to say it when asking someone's age in particular, since it can often come across as rude.

はじめまして | Nice to meet you

年齢を聞くのは失礼なんですね。
So it's rude to ask someone's age.

全員じゃないけど年齢を聞かれることが
嫌だと思う人はいると思うから、
聞くときには「失礼ですが…」をつけると、丁寧でいいよ。
Not for everyone, but I think there are people who don't like being asked about their age, so if you do ask, it's more polite and better to say "失礼ですが…"

失礼ですが、
ゆか先生の年齢をお伺いしてもよろしいでしょうか？
Excuse me, but can I ask your age, Yuka-sensei?

うーん…ひみつ！
Umm... it's a secret!

まとめ　年齢を聞くときは、特に丁寧に聞こう！
When asking someone's age, be especially polite!

丁寧な言い方　………　年齢をお伺いしてもよろしいでしょうか
Polite phrasing

「失礼ですが…」「差し支えなければ…」「もしよろしければ…」を前につけるともっといいよ！
It's even better to add "失礼ですが…" "差し支えなければ…" or "もしよろしければ…" before!

日本人のあいさつ

日本ではあいさつをするとき、お辞儀をします。そして、初めて会った人とあいさつをするときに、握手をすることはあまり多くありません。肩を組んだり、ハイタッチをしたりすることも、あまり多くはありませんね。日本人は他の国の人に比べて、相手の体を触ることにあまり慣れていないように感じます。それなのに、満員電車の中では痛いくらいに他人と体がぶつかります。そしてそれをみんな「当たり前」だと思っているんです。不思議ですよね。

Japanese greetings

When you greet someone in Japan, you bow. And when greeting someone you've met for the first time, it's not very common to shake hands. People don't often put their arms around each other's shoulders or give high fives, either. I feel like Japanese people are less accustomed to touching another person's body than people from other countries. Despite that, we bump into other people on crowded trains so much it almost hurts, and everyone thinks that's normal. Strange, isn't it?

あいさつ＆断り方
─ Greetings & How to say 'no' ─

ゆかちゃん、こんにちは！
Hello, Yuka-chan!

 [No.6]

⚠ ゆかちゃん、こんにちは！　Hello, Yuka-chan!

○ ゆかー！　Yuka-!

「こんにちは」は1番よく使うあいさつの言葉だと思っていたけど…。

I thought "こんにちは" was the most commonly used greeting...

あいさつには、「おはようございます」「こんにちは」「こんばんは」の3つがあるよね。
このあいさつ、実は友だちには全然言わないんだよ。
家族にも言わない！

There are three greetings: "おはようございます," "こんにちは,"
and "こんばんは."
Actually, people never say these greetings to friends.
You never say them to family, either!

えー！　そうなんですね！
じゃあ、なんて言えばいいんですか？

Huh! Is that so!
Then what should you say?

あいさつ＆断り方 | Greetings & How to say 'no'

学校や街で偶然友だちに会ったときは
「ゆかー！」って名前を呼ぶだけのことが多いよ。

When you happen to meet a friend at school or around town, you often just call them by their first name, like "Yuka!"

友だちには、「こんにちは」って言わないんですね。

So you don't say "こんにちは" to your friends.

そうだね。
「お！何してるの？」とか「ゆか！どこ行くの？」って
話しかけることも多いかな。
でも、「おはようございます」だけは、
「おはよう」って短くして友だちにも使うかな！

That's right.
I think it's common to start talking to them by saying things like "Oh! What are you up to?" Or "Yuka! Where are you going?"
But I suppose just "おはようございます" can be shortened to "おはよう" and used with friends!

まとめ 友だちには「こんにちは」って言わないよ！

Don't say "こんにちは" to your friends!

先生や近所の人など……………「おはようございます」「こんにちは」
For teachers, neighbors, and others　　「こんばんは」

友だち…………「おはよう」「名前（例：ゆかー！）」「少し話す（例：どこ行くの？）」など
For friends　　"おはよう," "First name (ex: Yuka!)," say a little something (ex: Where are you going?), etc.

⚠️ (会社で) こんにちは / こんばんは

(At the office) Hello. / Good evening.

- ⚠️ こんにちは。/ こんばんは。 Hello. / Good evening.
- 〇 お疲れ様です。 Good work today.

会社での基本的なあいさつは「お疲れ様です」。
「こんにちは」「こんばんは」は使わないかな。

"お疲れ様です (Good work today)" is the basic greeting used at the office. We don't say "こんにちは" or "こんばんは."

疲れていなくても、「お疲れ様です」って言わなければいけませんか？

Do you have to say "お疲れ様です" even if they aren't tired from putting in hard work?

そうだね。会社では疲れていなくても「お疲れ様です」と言おう！「お疲れ様です」という言葉は、本当に疲れているかどうかは関係なくて、「お仕事がんばっていますね。一緒にがんばりましょうね。」という気持ちがこもっている言葉だよ。

That's right. Use "お疲れ様です" at the office regardless! With the phrase "お疲れ様です," it doesn't matter whether you're really tired from putting in hard work or not. This phrase expresses that you see the other person is doing their best, and that you want to work hard together.

あいさつ & 断り方 | Greetings & How to say 'no'

いい言葉ですね。
That's a nice expression.

仕事が終わって帰るときは「お疲れ様でした」という言い方をすることが多いよ。
それから、会社でも「おはようございます」だけは使ってもいいんだ。朝会社にきたら、
まず「おはようございます」とあいさつしよう。

When going home after work, it's common to say "お疲れ様でした."
Also, of the three greetings, only "おはようございます" can be used at the office. When you get to work in the morning, say "おはようございます" first.

わかりました！
Understood!

まとめ　会社のあいさつは「お疲れ様です」
The greeting used at the office is "お疲れ様です"

基本のあいさつ ………… お疲れ様です
Basic greeting

朝会社にきたとき ………… おはようございます
Arriving at work in the morning

帰るとき ………… お疲れ様でした
Going home

⚠️ さようなら
Goodbye.

 [No.8]

⚠️ さようなら。 Goodbye.

○ ばいばーい！ Bye bye!

えー！ でも、先生はいつも「さようなら」って言いますよね？
Huh! But teachers always say "さようなら," right?

「さようなら」は、学校の先生が家に帰る学生によく使う言葉なんだ。
でも実は、日常生活で「さようなら」と言うことはほとんどないよ。
特に、友だちには絶対に使わないよ。

"さようなら" is a word that school teachers often say to students who are going home.
But actually, it's rare to say "さようなら" in everyday life.
It's never used with friends in particular.

えー！ そうなんですか…。
正しい言葉だと思っていました…。
Huh! Is that so...
I thought that was the right word to use...

034

あいさつ＆断り方｜Greetings & How to say 'no'

間違いではないよ。
でも、「さようなら」という言葉は「これからも、ずっとさようなら」というような意味を感じます。
だから、ドラマや映画の恋人と別れるシーンで「あなたとはもう付き合えないわ。さようなら。」
こういうセリフをよく聞くと思います。

It's not incorrect.
But the word "さようなら" feels like it means "goodbye forever."
That's why in TV show and movies scenes when a character breaks up with their lover, you often hear lines like "I can't be with you anymore. さようなら"

じゃあ友だちには何と言って別れますか？
So then what do you say when you split up with your friends?

友だちには「ばいばーい！」「じゃあね！」「また明日！」と言うことが多いかな。

I think people often say "ばいばーい!" "じゃあね!" or "また明日!"

まとめ 「さようなら」は「ずっとさようなら」という感じがする！

"さようなら" sounds like "Goodbye forever"!

友だち ……………「ばいばーい」「じゃあね」「また明日」
For friends

先生と学生 …………「さようなら」
Between teachers and students

⚠️ どういたしまして
You're welcome.

- ⚠️ どういたしまして。 You're welcome.
- ◯ うん。 Yeah.

「ありがとう」と「どういたしまして」はセットですよね？
"ありがとう" and "どういたしまして" come as a set, right?

お礼（れい）を言（い）われたときに「どういたしまして」と言うのは正（ただ）しいし、もちろん使（つか）ってもOK。でも実（じつ）は、友（とも）だちにはあまり言わないよ。「どういたしまして」はちょっと丁寧（ていねい）すぎる感（かん）じがしてしまうんだ。

Saying "どういたしまして" when someone thanks you is correct, and it's of course fine to use this phrase. But actually, you don't really say it to friends. "どういたしまして" feels a bit too polite.

なるほど。じゃあ何（なん）と言（い）いますか？
I see. Then what would you say?

友（とも）だちに「ありがとう」と言（い）われたときは、「うん」と言えば十分（じゅうぶん）。「うん」「ううん」「はーい」こんなふうに返事（へんじ）をすることが多（おお）いよ。

When a friend says "ありがとう," just saying "うん" is enough.
It's common to reply like "うん" "ううん" or "はーい"

あいさつ & 断り方 | Greetings & How to say 'no'

友だち以外だったら、何と言うことが多いですか？
If the person's not your friend, what do people often to say?

友だち以外なら、「いいえ」「いえいえ」「はい」
「とんでもないです」こんな返事をすることが多いよ。
If they're not your friend, people often reply with things like
"いいえ," "いえいえ" "はい" or "とんでもないです"

なるほど。先生ありがとうございます！
I see. Thank you, sensei!

いいえ！役に立ったかな？
いいえ! Did that help?

まとめ

「どういたしまして」より自然な言い方がある！

There's more natural ways to say "どういたしまして"!

友だち ……………「うん」「ううん」「はーい」
For friends

友だち以外 ………「いいえ」「いえいえ」「はい」「とんでもないです」
For others

⚠ すみません、ちょっと…
Sorry, it's a bit...

⚠ すみません、ちょっと… Sorry, it's a bit...

○ **すみません + 理由 + お礼** Sorry + reason + thanks

例文 Example sentence
すみません、今日は用事があるので行けません。でも、ありがとうございます。

この断り方、初級で勉強しましたね。
日本人ははっきりと断ることがあまりないので、
1番いい断り方なんじゃないですか？

We learned this way of saying no in elementary Japanese. Japanese people don't say no clearly, so isn't this the best way to refuse something?

そうなんだけど、少しあいまいすぎるかな。
「今日、飲みに行こうよ！」と誘われたら「すみません、今日は用事があるので行けません。」と言えばいいよ。

That's right, but I think it's a little too vague.
If someone says "Let's go drinking today!" and invites you out, you can say "すみません, I can't go because I have something to do today."

思ったより、はっきり断るんですね。
So people say no more clearly than I'd thought.

あいさつ & 断り方｜Greetings & How to say 'no'

「すみません、ちょっと…」と言われたら、「ちょっと…何?」と思うよね。理由を言ってはっきり断れば、相手も嫌な気持ちにならないはず。

If someone says "すみません、ちょっと…" you would think "A bit... what?" If you say no clearly and with a reason, the other person shouldn't feel uncomfortable.

なるほど。その方が丁寧な返事ですね。

I see. So that's a more polite way to reply.

そして最後に、お礼の気持ちも伝えよう。「すみません、今日は用事があるので…。お誘いいただきありがとうございます。」と「すみません + 理由 + お礼」を言うといいね。「また誘ってください」のように前向きな言葉を付け加えて言うのもいいと思う。

And lastly, express your thanks.
It's good to say "すみません + a reason + thanks", like "すみません、I have something to do today. Thanks for inviting me." I think it's also good to add something proactive, like "Please invite me again next time."

まとめ 「すみません、ちょっと…」よりいい言い方がある!

There's a better way to say no than "すみません、ちょっと…"!

おすすめの言い方 ……… すみません + 理由 + お礼

Recommended phrasing   すみません + reason + thanks

⚠️ 結構です
It's fine.

⚠️ 結構です。 It's fine.

🔵 ありがとうございます。でも大丈夫です。 Thank you. But it's okay.

これって、丁寧な断り方じゃないんですか？
Isn't this a polite way of saying no?

言い方にもよるんだけど、ちょっと冷たい印象があるかな。
It depends on how you say it, but I think it comes off a bit cold.

そうなんですか。
Is that so?

これも、「ありがとうございます」などのお礼の言葉と一緒に使えば印象は大きく変わるよ。
「ありがとうございます、でも結構です」や「大丈夫です」と言うのもいいよ。「大丈夫です」は「結構です」と同じ意味だけど、もっとやわらかい言葉だからね。

The impression changes a lot with this phrase too if you use it together with words of gratitude like "ありがとうございます." You can also say "ありがとうございます、でも結構です" or "大丈夫です." "大丈夫です" has the same meaning as "結構です," but it's more gentle.

あいさつ & 断り方 | Greetings & How to say 'no'

「結構です」と言うことはないんですか？
People don't say "結構です"?

例えばお店で何か商品を強くおすすめされて
「これすごくいいですよ！買いませんか？」と
言われたときは、「結構です」と言うことが多いよ。
「本当に必要ありません」と言いたいときには、
「結構です」はぴったりな言葉なんだ。

For example, when a store clerk says "This product is really good! Would you like to buy it?" and is strongly pushing something, people often say "結構です."
結構です" is the perfect word when you want to say that you really don't need something.

まとめ

「結構です」は少し冷たい印象がある断り方！
"結構です" is a slightly cold way of saying no!

おすすめの断り方……「お礼 + でも結構です」「大丈夫です」
Recommended phrasing

日本人のラーメンの食べ方

みなさんは日本のラーメンが好きですか？私は大好き！日本でラーメンを食べたことがある人ならわかると思うのですが、日本人はラーメンを食べるとき「ずるずるっ！」と音を立てて食べます。すごくうるさいんですよね。食事中は音を立てないように静かにご飯を食べている日本人ですが、ラーメンは特別です。「えー！」と思う人もいるかもしれませんが、ラーメンは音を立てて勢いよく食べた方がおいしいし、いい食べ方だと思っている人が多いです。これも不思議ですよね。

How to eat Japanese ramen

Do you like Japanese ramen? I love it! As anyone who's eaten ramen in Japan would know, Japanese people make a slurping sound when eating it. It's really loud, right? Japanese people eat quietly so as not to make noise during meals, but ramen is a special case. Some of you might be surprised, but lots of people think it's good and that ramen tastes better when you slurp with force and make noise. This is strange too, isn't it?

日常会話
にちじょうかいわ
― Daily conversation ―

今ひまですか？
Are you free right now?

 [No.12]

⚠ 今ひまですか？　Are you free right now?

○ 今お時間よろしいでしょうか？　Do you have time right now?

「ひま」は「仕事をしていない」という印象がある言葉だから、先生や上司に「ひまですか？」と言うのはやめた方がいいよ。

"ひま" is a word that gives an impression that you're not working, so you should stop asking your teacher or boss "ひまですか？"

じゃあ、どうやって聞いたらいいですか？

Then how should I ask them that?

「今お時間よろしいでしょうか」と聞こう。先生がとてもひまそうにしていても、「ひまですか？」って聞かないでね！

Ask them "今お時間よろしいでしょうか？"
Even if your teacher looks like they're really free, don't ask "ひまですか？"!

めんどくさいな〜。同じ意味なのに…。

How annoying... Even though they mean the same thing...

日常会話 | Daily conversation

そうだよね。でも、相手が受けるあなたへの印象がすごくよくなると思うよ！「ひまですか？」って聞かれたら、「失礼な人だな」と思ってしまう。

That's right. But the impression you give the other person will be better. If you ask "ひまですか？", many people will feel like you're a rude person.

確かにそうですね。

That's certainly true.

でしょ？実は「ゆか先生、今ひまですか？」は、私が学生からよく言われる言葉なんだ。私は全然嫌な気持ちにならないけど、「これを他の日本人に言っていたら、みんなが損をしてしまうな…」と思ったんだ。ちなみに、友だちに「今ひま？」と聞くのはすごく自然な言い方だから、使ってもまったく問題ないよ。

Right? Actually, students often say "ゆか先生、今ひまですか？" to me. It doesn't bother me at all, but I've thought that if students were to say this to other Japanese people, everybody would lose out... By the way, "今ひま？" is a really natural thing to ask friends, so it's perfectly fine to use it.

まとめ 「今ひまですか？」と目上の人に聞くのはすごく失礼！

Asking your superiors "今ひまですか？" is really rude!

先生や上司……「今お時間よろしいでしょうか？」
For teacher and bosses

友だち……「今ひま？」と聞いてもOK！
For friends　　　It's OK to ask "今ひま？"!

⚠ お菓子がほしいですか？
Do you want some sweets?

> ⚠ **お菓子がほしいですか？** Do you want some sweets？
>
> ○ **お菓子はいかがですか？** How would you like some sweets？

 [No.13]

「ほしいですか」って初級で勉強しますよね。どうして失礼なんですか？

Students learn "ほしいですか" at the elementary level. Why is it rude?

「〜がほしいですか」は、相手のほしい物ややりたいことを聞くときに使う文法だよね。でも、これを先生や上司に対して使うと少し失礼な印象になってしまうよ。

"〜がほしいですか" is a grammar point used to ask about things the other person wants or what they want to do. But using this with teachers and bosses gives off a bit of a rude impression.

え？ そうなんですか？

Huh? Is that so?

うん。目上の人に欲望を直接聞くことは、日本語では失礼な印象になることが多いんだ。

Yeah. Asking your superiors about their desires directly often gives off a rude impression in Japanese.

日常会話 | Daily conversation

でも、どうしても目上の人に何がほしいか、何がしたいかを聞きたいときはどうするんですか？

But what do you do when you really want to ask your superiors what they want or what they want to do?

どうしても「〜がほしい、〜がしたい」を使わないと言いたいことが伝わらない場面なら、使っていいよ！でも、だいたいのことは別の言い方ができると思うから探してみて。「〜はいかがですか」「〜はどうですか」「どれがお好みですか」などなど、たくさんあるよ！

If you can't convey what you want to say without using "〜がほしい、〜がしたい" it's fine to use it! But I think most things have different ways they can be phrased, so try finding some! There are many different expressions, like "〜はいかがですか（How would you like…），" "〜はどうですか（How about…），" and "どれがお好みですか（Which do you prefer?）" and more!

まとめ

目上の人に「〜がほしいですか・したいですか」と聞くのは失礼！

Asking your superiors "〜がほしいですか・したいですか" is rude!

- 欲望を直接聞くのは失礼になることがある。
  It can be rude to directly ask about someone's desires.

- 「○○が飲みたいですか」
  →「○○はいかがですか」のように、別の言い方を探そう
  Find another way to phrase it, like "○○が飲みたいですか（Do you want to drink XX?）"
  → "○○はいかがですか（How would you like XX?）"

⚠ 上手ですね
じょうず

You're good at that.

⚠ 上手ですね。　You're good at that.

○ すごいですね！　You're amazing!

この前、学生に「ゆか先生は上手に教えました！ありがとう！」とほめてもらったんだ。
すごくうれしかったんだけど、少し違和感があったんだ。

The other day, I had a student compliment me, saying "ゆか先生は上手に教えました！ありがとう！(Yuka-sensei, you taught us well today! Thank you!)" I was really happy to hear it, but it felt a bit weird.

プロに「上手」と言うのが失礼ということですね。

So it's rude to say a professional is "上手(good at)" something.

いつも失礼になるわけじゃないよ。でも、例えば私が歌手に対して「歌が上手ですね」って言うのは失礼だね。「プロなんだから上手に決まってるでしょ！それでお金をもらっているんだから！」って思われると思う。「上手ですね」と言うと、相手のことを評価しているような感じがするよ。

It isn't always rude. But it'd be rude to say to a singer, for example, "歌が上手ですね(You're good at singing)" I think they'd think "Of course I'm good at it, I'm a professional! That's why I'm getting paid!" When you say "上手ですね" it feels like you're assessing the other person.

日常会話 | Daily conversation

「上手」を使わないほめ方はありますか？
Are there ways to compliment someone that don't use "上手"?

「上手ですね」の代わりに
「いや〜！ さすがですね！ 本当にすごいです！」
のように、自分が感動している気持ちを表す言葉を使うと、ほめたいという気持ちがよく伝わるよ。

If you use words that express your emotions, like "Wow! As expected! You're really amazing!" instead of "上手ですね" you can easily convey that you want to compliment them.

ゆか先生、さすがです！
As expected, Yuka-sensei!

まとめ

「上手」は使う場面に注意しよう！
Be careful when using "上手"!

上手ですね ……… プロに言うのはよくない
You're good at that / Not good to say to a professional

すごい！さすが！ …… ほめたい気持ちを伝えることができる
Amazing! As expected! / Can convey that you want to give a compliment

⚠️ 先生にお菓子を買ってあげます

I'll buy sweets for you, sensei.

⚠️ **先生にお菓子を買ってあげます。**
I'll buy sweets for you, sensei.

○ **先生、お菓子はいかがですか。**
Sensei, how would you like some sweets?

[No.15]

これも失礼なんですか…。
最初に勉強したのになぁ。
Is this rude too?
Even though we learned this in the beginning…

そうだね。
「〜をあげる」とか「〜してあげる」という言い方は、
基本的にする人がしてあげる人よりも
上に立っている印象がある言葉なんだ。
だから、先生や上司に「ジュースを買ってあげますよ！」と言うと失礼だよ。

That's right. Phrases like "〜をあげる" and "〜してあげる" basically give the impression that the person who doing it is above the other person. That's why it's rude to say "ジュースを買ってあげますよ！" to your teacher or boss.

じゃあ、何と言えばいいんですか？
Then what should you say?

日常会話 | Daily conversation

「差し上げます」を使うとすごく丁寧だよ。
でも日常会話では「ジュースはいかがですか？」とか
「ジュース飲まれますか？」という聞き方が自然だね。

It's very polite to use "差し上げます (I will give you ～)." But in everyday conversation, it's natural to ask "ジュースはいかがですか(How would you like some juice?)" or "ジュース飲まれますか(Would you like to drink juice)?"

気をつけないとな…。
I've got to be careful...

友だち同士なら「これ買ってあげる」とか
「教えてあげる」とか「私がやってあげる」のように、
日常会話でもよく使うよ。

With friends, you'll often use phrases in everyday conversation like "これ買ってあげる(I'll buy this for you,)" "私がやってあげる(I'll teach you/tell you,)" or "これ買ってあげる(I'll do it for you.)"

まとめ

「あげます」は、あげる人があげる相手より上に立つ言葉！

The phrase "あげます" means the speaker is above the other person!

「○○をあげます」
→「○○はいかがですか」「○○を差し上げます」

※友だちには「〜あげる」と言っても問題なし

※No problem saying "〜あげる" to friends.

⚠ あー、はいはい
Ah, yes, yes.

 [No.16]

⚠ あー、はいはい。　Ah, yes, yes.

○ はい。　Yes.

「はい」って、たくさん言ったら失礼ですか？
Is it rude to say "はい" a lot?

そう！ すごく失礼！
Yes! Really rude!

もし、先生に対して「はいはい」と返事をしたら、どう思われますか？
What would you think if someone replied "はいはい" to you?

話をちゃんと聞いてない、真面目にやろうとしていない、と思うね。印象はすごく悪いよ。
I'd think they haven't listened to what I've said properly and aren't taking things seriously. It gives a really bad impression.

えー！ 1回「はい」が多いだけで、そんなに印象が悪くなりますか？
Huh! Does the impression really worsen that much with just one extra "はい"?

日常会話 | Daily conversation

そうだね。すごく失礼だから相手を怒らせてしまうこともあると思う。
先生や上司には「はい」は1度だけ言おうね。

That's right. It's really rude, so I think it'll make the other person angry. Say "はい" only once to your teachers and bosses.

はーい！

はーい!

それ！「はーい」と伸ばして言うのもよくないよ。
「はいはい」と同じように、適当に返事をしている印象になってしまう。目上の人への返事は、短く大きな声で「はい！」わかった？

That too! It's not good to stretch the "はい." Just like "はいはい" it gives the impression that you're responding half-heartedly. To your superiors, reply with a short "はい！" in a loud voice. Got it?

はい！！（めんどくさいな！）

はい!! (How annoying!)

まとめ　「はい」は1度だけ！

Say "はい" only once!

いい言い方 ……「はい！」
Proper phrasing

悪い言い方 ……「はいはい」
Poor phrasing 　　　　「はーい」

⚠️ 愛しています
I love you

 [No.17]

⚠️ 愛しています。　I love you

○ 大好きだよ。いつもありがとう。　I really like you. Thank you for everything.

実は日本人は「愛してる」って全然言わないんだよね。
愛情を伝えるときには「好き」とか「大好き」とか、
違う言葉を使うんだ。

Japanese people actually don't every say "愛してる (I love you)."
We use different words such as "好き(like)" and "大好き(really like)"
when communicating their love.

えー！じゃあ I love you ってどうやって伝えるんですか？

Huh! So how do you tell someone "I love you"?

日本人の感覚としては、I love you が「大好きだよ」
と同じくらいの言葉だと思うんだよね。
「愛してる」は言葉が重すぎる。
プロポーズのときなら言うんじゃないかな？

I think that from a Japanese perspective, the English "I love you" is on
the same level as "大好きだよ" The word "愛してる" is too strong. People
might say it when they propose, I guess.

日常会話 | Daily conversation

「愛してる」ってあんまり使わない言葉なんですね。
So "愛してる" isn't a world people use often.

私はまだ言ったことないなぁ。他にも、日本人は「ありがとう」という言葉で愛情を表現することがよくあるよ。「いつも一緒にいてくれてありがとう」「そばにいてくれてありがとう」とかね。
I've never said it yet. Besides, Japanese people often express their affection by saying "ありがとう(Thank you)" When people say "Thank you for always being with me" or "Thank you for being by my side" and so on.

へえー！ でもやっぱり「愛してる」って聞きたいですよね♡
Wow! But as I thought, I still want to hear "愛してる" ♡

私も言われてみたいな♡
I want to be told that too ♡

まとめ 愛情を伝えるときは「好き」「大好き」を使おう！
Use "好き" and "大好き" when communicating your love!

「ありがとう」とたくさんのお礼の気持ちを伝えることも、愛情表現の1つ
Saying "ありがとう" and conveying lots of gratitude is another way to express your love

ゆか先生とあやの先生の出会い

Yuka-sensei and Ayano-sensei's encounter

はじめまして！**佐藤あやのです。**
どうぞ、よろしくお願いします。

Nice to meet you! I'm Ayano Sato.
Pleasure to meet you.

はじめまして。**よろしく〜！**
何かわからんことあったら、何でも聞いてなー。

Nice to meet you. It's a pleasure〜！
If you've got any questions, ask away.

はい！えっと、ゆか先生って**どちらの方なんですか**？

Sure! Umm, where are you from, Yuka-sensei?

出身？関西やで。神戸！

Where I was born? Kansai. In Kobe!

やっぱり、そうなんですね。
すごい関西弁だったのでびっくりしました。

That's what I thought. I was surprised because you spoke with so much Kansai dialect.

せやんなぁ。授業のときがんばって関西弁を話さないようにしているから…。
Right... That's because I try my best not to speak in Kansai dialect during class...

あと…失礼ですが、ゆか先生の年齢をお伺いしてもよろしいでしょうか？
And excuse me, but could I ask your age?

28歳やで。一緒ぐらい？
I'm 28. About the same as you?

はい、私はゆか先生の2つ下です！
Yes, I'm two years younger than you!

あやの先生はYouTubeの私の動画を見て
「こんなふうに日本語を教えたい！」と言って
「日本語の森」に来てくれたんだ。
すごい行動力だよね！
今では「日本語の森」の大切な仲間だよ。
Ayano-sensei joined 'Nihongo no Mori' after she watched my videos on YouTube and thought "I want to teach Japanese like this!" Such initiative, right! Now, she's an important member of 'Nihongo no Mori.'

会話 ①-2 仕事のあとは、かんぱい！
A toast after work!

 [No.19]

お疲れー！
Good job today!

あ、お疲れ様です！
ゆか先生、今お時間よろしいでしょうか？
Oh, thanks for your hard work today! Yuka-sensei, do you have a moment now?

うん。どうしたの？
Yeah. What's going on?

明日の授業の準備してたんですけど、ゆか先生はこの文法いつもどんな感じで説明してますか？
I was preparing for tomorrow's class, but how do you always explain this grammar point?

うーん、これ難しいよね。
Umm, this one's difficult, isn't it.

そうなんですよ…。
Right...

まあ、とりあえずビール飲みに行く？
それは、明日考えようよ！

Well, want to go out for beer for now? Let's think about it tomorrow!

え、でも…すみません、
今日は用事があるので行けません。
また明日行きましょう。

Huh, but... I can't go out because I have something to do today.
Let's go tomorrow.

用事って、どうせ仕事でしょー？

By 'something' you mean work anyway, right?

はい…まだ資料の作成が終わってなくて…。

Yes... I haven't finished creating my materials yet...

やっぱり！はい、今日は仕事終わり！ほら！飲みに行こう！

That's what I thought! Alright, work's over for today! See! Let's go for a drink!

いつも2人で相談をしながら授業の準備をしているよ。
あやの先生は本当にいつも一生懸命！
仕事の後は、よく一緒にお酒を飲みに行くんだ。

We always consult each other while preparing for lessons.
Ayano-sensei always works really hard!
After work, we go out for drinks a lot together.

北海道出身のあやの先生
Ayano-sensei from Hokkaido

[No.20]

ゆか先生！
北海道の実家からとうきびがたくさん届いたんです！
おひとついかがですか？

Yuka-sensei! I got a lot of toukibi sent to me from home back in Hokkaido! Would you like one?

とうきびって何？

What is toukibi?

とうもろこしのことですよー！はい、どうぞ。

It's corn! Here you are.

めっちゃおいしそう〜！ありがとう！

It looks super good! Thanks!

いえいえ。すっごく甘いですよ。

No problem. It's really sweet.

私とうもろこし食べるのめっちゃ早いんだ。いくよ？（パクパクパク…）

I eat corn super quickly. Ready? (Munch munch munch...)

わー！ ゆか先生すごいですね！
Wow! Yuka-sensei, you're amazing!

でしょ？
Right?

そんなにお好きなら、もう1本差し上げますよ！
If you like corn so much, I'll give you another one!

いや、1本で大丈夫。ありがとう。
No, one is fine. Thanks.

そうですか…。
Is that so...

私は関西出身だけど、
あやの先生は北海道出身なんだ！
北海道の言葉はほとんど東京と同じなんだけど、
言い方が違うものもあるよ。

I'm from Kansai, but Ayano-sensei is from Hokkaido!
The words used in Hokkaido are mostly the same as Tokyo,
but there are some that are different.

日本人が漢字を勉強する方法

　みなさんは漢字が好きですか？「日本人はどうやって漢字を覚えるんですか？」と聞かれることが多いのですが、日本人の漢字の覚え方はそんなに特別なものではありません。日本では小学校1年生から漢字の勉強が始まります。漢字の書き方を学校で勉強したあと「漢字ノート」という四角がたくさん並んでいるノートに、漢字を何度も書きます。これが宿題です。同じ漢字を何度も何度も紙に書いて覚えるんです。手が痛くなるし、鉛筆のせいで黒くなるし、大変なんですよね。たくさん覚えた後は、漢字のテストもあります。日本人もみなさんと同じように苦労して漢字を勉強するんですよ。また、日本の学校では漢字の「書き順」も習います。鉛筆で文字を書くときはあまりわからないと思いますが、筆で文字を書くときは正しい書き順で書かないと美しい文字を書くのが難しいです。

　みなさんは「漢字検定」という試験を知っていますか？ JLPTのように1級、2級とレベルが分かれている試験です。難しいレベルだと日本人でもちゃんと勉強しないとわからない漢字がたくさん出題されます。漢字が大好きだ！という人がいれば受けてみると面白いかもしれませんね。

How Japanese people learn kanji

Do you like kanji? People often ask me how Japanese people learn kanji, but it's not that special. In Japan, kids start studying kanji from first grade. After learning how to write kanji at school, we write them over and over in a "Kanji Notebook" that has lots of squares lined up. That's our homework. We learn kanji by writing them down on paper again and again. Your hand hurts and turns black from the pencil. Tough, right? After learning lots of kanji, there's also a test. Japanese people have a hard time studying kanji, just like you. And we also learn the "stroke order" of each kanji at school. It's hard to understand when writing kanji with a pencil, but when writing with a brush, it's difficult to draw beautiful characters unless you write them with the proper stroke order.

Do you know about a test called the "漢字検定(Kanji Kentei)"? Like the JLPT, it's a test that is divided into levels like 1-kyu and 2-kyu (level 1/2). At higher difficulty levels, there are lots of questions about kanji that even Japanese people don't know without proper study. If any of you love kanji, you might be interested in taking it.

これってどういうこと?
意味がややこしい言葉

What does this mean?
Words with complicated meanings

● P.65〜 　意味がいっぱいある言葉
　　　　　Words with Lots of Meanings

● P.79〜 　教科書と意味が違う言葉
　　　　　Words with Different Textbook Definitions

● P.87〜 　違いがややこしい言葉
　　　　　Words with Tricky Differences

● P.95〜 　意味がややこしい言い方
　　　　　Words with Complicated Meanings

2章、はじまるよ!

意味がいっぱいある言葉

― Words with Lots of Meanings ―

大丈夫
だいじょうぶ
Fine / No problem / Not necessary

「大丈夫」には3つの意味があります。
"大丈夫" has three meanings.

[1] 平気 Fine / Okay  [No.21]

「体調悪そうだね。**大丈夫**？」
「ちょっと頭が痛いんだ。でも、**大丈夫**。」

"You look sick. Are you okay?"
"I've got a bit of a headache. But I'm fine."

Q いつ使う？ When do you use it?

A 体調が悪い人とか、困っている人のことを心配しているときに使うよ。
You use it when you're worried about someone who's sick or in trouble.

Q 言われた人は、なんて答える？
What would someone say when asked this?

A 平気じゃないときも「大丈夫」と言うことが多いかな。
People probably often say "大丈夫" even if they're not.

Q どうして…？ How come...?

A 心配をかけたくないから「大丈夫」と言う人が多いと思う。
I think lots of people say "大丈夫" because they don't want to make people worry.

Q じゃあ、どうして「大丈夫？」と聞くの？
Then why would you ask "大丈夫"?

A 「心配しているよ」という気持ちを伝えたいからだよ。
Because we want to let them know we're feeling worried about them.

意味がいっぱいある言葉 | Words with Lots of Meanings

[2] 問題ない No problem 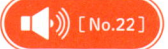 [No.22]

「飲み会、明日の予定だけど**大丈夫**？」
"The drinking party is scheduled for tomorrow, are you okay to come?"

「はい！**大丈夫**です！」
"Yes! No problem!"

Q いつ使う？
When do you use it?

A 何かを相手に確認したいときに使うよ。
You use it when you want to confirm something with the other person.

Q じゃあ、最初の会話はどんな意味？
So what does the first conversation mean?

A 他の言葉で言うと、こんな感じ！↓

「飲み会は明日だけど、行けるよね？覚えてるよね？」

「問題ないですよ、参加できますよ。」

In other words, it's like this! ↓
"The drinking party is tomorrow, you can come, right? You remember, right?"
"No problem, I can join"

今日の夜、大丈夫？
Are you okay to come tonight?

大丈夫ー。
Tonight's fine.

[3] 必要ない　Not necessary

「おはしはお付けしましょうか？」
「あ、**大丈夫**です。」

"Shall I include chopsticks?"
"Oh, not necessary."

Q いつ使う？
　　When do you use it?

A 断りたいときに使うよ。
　　You use it when you want to turn down something.

Q じゃあ、最初の会話はどんな意味？
　　So what does the first conversation mean?

A 他の言葉で言うと、こんな感じ！↓
　　「おはしは必要ですか？」
　　「あ、いらないです。必要ないです。」

　　In other words, it's like this! ↓
　　"Do you need chopsticks?"
　　"Oh, I don't need them. They're not necessary."

Q どうして「いらないです」って言わないの？
　　How come wouldn't you say "いらないです"?

A 「大丈夫です」と言って断った方が、やわらかい印象になるからかな。
　　「ありがとう、でも必要ないんだ」という意味になるよ。

　　I think it's because it sounds softer to decline by saying "大丈夫です."
　　It means "Thanks, but I don't need it."

まとめ

「大丈夫」を使う場面は3つあるよ！
There are 3 situations when you can use "大丈夫!"

[1] 人を心配するとき / されたときの「大丈夫」
"大丈夫" when worried about people/they're worried about you

[2] 確認するときの「大丈夫」
"大丈夫" when checking something

[3] 断るときの「大丈夫」
"大丈夫" when refusing something

例文で確認！

[1] かぜって聞いたけど、大丈夫？──大丈夫！生きてるよ〜！
I heard you have a cold, are you okay? ── I'm fine! Still alive!

[2] 明日家に行っても大丈夫？──うん、大丈夫だよ！
Is it okay to go over to your house tomorrow? ── Yeah, no problem!

[3] 駅まで送ろうか？──大丈夫。ありがとう！
Shall I send you off to the station? ── You don't have to. Thanks!

いいです
Good / No problem / Not necessary

「いいです」には3つの意味があります。
"いいです" has three meanings.

[1] いい　Good / Nice

「この服、昨日買ったんだ。」
「**いいね！** すごく似合ってるよ。」

"I bought this outfit yesterday."
"Nice! It looks great on you."

Q いつ使う？
When do you use it?

A 人をほめるときとか、感想を言うときに使うよ。
You use it when complimenting people or giving your thoughts.

Q この「いい」はどんな意味？
What does "いい" mean here?

A 「よい」と相手をほめる意味だよ。SNSにも「いいね！」というボタンがあるよ。
It means complimenting the other person, saying something's "nice/good." It's also used as the "いいね！(Like!)" button on social media.

 そのバッグ**いいね**！ かわいい！ 似合ってる！
That bag looks good! So cute! It suits you!

ありがとう！ ゆか先生にもらったんだー！
Thank you! I got it from Yuka-sensei!

意味がいっぱいある言葉 | Words with Lots of Meanings

[2] 問題ない No problem  [No.25]

「このお菓子、食べて**いい**？」 "Can I eat this candy?"

「うん、**いい**よ。」 "Yeah, no problem."

Q いつ使う？
When do you use it?

A 相手に確認したり、許可をとるときに使うよ。
You use it to confirm something with the other person or get permission.

Q じゃあ、最初の会話はどんな意味？
So what does the first conversation mean?

A 他の言葉で言うと、こんな感じ！↓
「このお菓子、食べて問題ないですか？」
「うん、食べて問題ないよ。」

In other words, it's like this! ↓
"Is it okay to eat this candy?"
"Yeah, no problem for you to eat it."

Q 返事は「いい」だけじゃダメなの？
You can't just respond with "いい"?

A 返事は「いい」だけじゃなくて、「いいよ」とか「いいです」と言った方が自然だよ。
It's more natural to say "いいよ" or "いいです" instead of just saying "いい."

Q 「このお菓子、食べて大丈夫？」と聞いてもいいの？
Can I ask "Is it okay（大丈夫）to eat this candy?"

A そういう聞き方でもOK。でも、「食べて大丈夫？」って聞いたら、「くさってない？」とか「食べてだれかに怒られない？」とか、「これを食べることで起こる問題」がないかどうかを聞く意味にもなるよ。

That way of asking is OK, too. But asking "Is it okay（大丈夫）to eat?" also means you're asking, "Has it gone bad?" "Will someone get angry at me for eating this?" or "Will it cause any problems for me to eat this?"

[3] 必要ない Not necessary

「仕事、手伝おうか？」 "Shall I help?"
「いや、**いいです。**」 "No, I'm good."

Q いつ使う？ When do you use it?

A 断るときに使うよ。 You will use it when refusing something.

Q じゃあ、最初の会話はどんな意味？ So what does the first conversation mean?

A 他の言葉で言うと、こんな感じ！↓　　In other words, it's like this! ↓
「あなたの仕事を手伝いましょうか？」 "Would you like me to help you with your work?"
「いいえ、手伝わなくていいです。」 "No, you don't have to help."

Q 返事は「いい」だけじゃダメなの？ You can't just respond with "いい"?

A 返事は「いい」だけじゃなくて、「いいよ」とか「いいです」と言う方が自然だよ。
It's more natural to say "いいよ" or "いいです" instead of just saying "いい."

Q 反対の意味になるってとても難しい…日本人はみんな、正しく意味を理解できているの？
It's so difficult how it can have the opposite meaning.
Can all Japanese people understand the meaning correctly?

A 日本人でも、わからないときがあるよ！
例えばコンビニで買い物をしたときに、店員さんが「食べ物と一緒におはしを入れてもいいですか？」と聞いてくることがあるんだ。そのときに「いいです」とだけ返事をすると「一緒におはしを入れて『いい』」のか「おはしは『いらない』」のか、はっきりわからなくなってしまうよ。そういうときは、表情やジェスチャーがすごく大切になるんだ。
Sometimes even Japanese people don't understand!
Like when shopping at a convenience store, the clerk will sometime ask, "Is it okay to put chopsticks in with your food?" At that time, if you just reply "いいです," you wouldn't be able to clearly tell whether "it's 'fine' to put in the chopsticks" or "it's 'not necessary'" to put in the chopsticks". At times like that, facial expressions and gestures are super important.

意味がいっぱいある言葉 | Words with Lots of Meanings

まとめ

「いいです」を使う場面は3つあるよ！
There are 3 situations when you use "いいです"!

[1] 人をほめるときの「いいですね！」
"いいですね！" when complimenting people

[2] 許可をとるときの「いいですか？」
"いいですか？" when getting permission

[3] 断るときの「いいです。」
"いいです" when refusing something

例文で確認！

[1] 今から焼肉、食べに行かない？ ── いいね！行こう行こう！
Wanna go have yakiniku now? ── Nice! Let's go, let's go!

[2] ちょっと手伝ってもらっていい？ ── うん。何をすればいいの？
Could you help me out a bit? ── Sure. What should I do?

[3] 今日みんなで飲みに行くんだけど、来るよね？ ── いや、私はいいです。
We're all going out for drinks today. You're coming, right? ── No, I'm good.

すみません
I'm sorry / Thank you / Excuse me

「すみません」には3つの意味があります。
"すみません" has three meanings.

[1] ごめんなさい I'm sorry

「ちょっと静かにしていただけますか。」 "Could you please be a little quieter?"
「はい、**すみません**。」 "Sure, I'm sorry."

Q いつ使う？ When do you use it?

A あやまるときに使うよ。You use it when apologizing for something.

Q 「ごめんなさい」や「申し訳ございません」とはどう違うの？
How is it different from "ごめんなさい" or "申し訳ございません"?

A どれも意味は同じで、あやまるときに使う言葉なんだ。でも「ごめんなさい」の方が相手に許してもらいたいという気持ちが強く伝わるよ。それと、子どもは「すみません」をほとんど使わないね。「申し訳ありません」はとても丁寧な言い方だから、会社でよく使うよ。「すみません」はあやまるときによく使う言葉だけど、例文のように人から注意されて少しあやまるなら、「すみません」が1番ぴったりなんだ。

They all mean the same thing and are words you use when apologizing. But "ごめんなさい" conveys a strong desire for the other person to forgive you. And children rarely use "すみません." "申し訳ありません" is a very polite way of saying "I'm sorry," so it's used at work a lot. "すみません" is a word that's used often when apologizing, although if you're apologizing after someone's said something to you like in the example, "すみません" is the best choice.

Q 使えない場面はある？
Are there any situations when you can't use it?

A どんな場面で使っても、失礼じゃないよ。
It wouldn't be rude to use it in any kind of situation.

意味がいっぱいある言葉 | Words with Lots of Meanings

[2] ありがとう　Thank you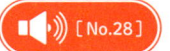

「お土産を買ってきましたよ。どうぞ。」 "I bought you a souvenir. Here you go."

「**すみません**。いただきます。」　"Thank you. I really appreciate it."

Q いつ使う？
When do you use it?

A 人にお礼を言うときに使うよ。
You use it when thanking people.

Q じゃあ、最初の会話はどんな意味？
So what does the first conversation mean?

A 他の言葉で言うと、こんな感じ！↓

「お土産を買ってきましたよ。どうぞ。」
「私のために買ってきてくれて、ありがとうございます。いただきます。」

In other words, it's like this! ↓
"I bought you a souvenir. Here you go."
"Thank you for buying this for me. I really appreciate it."

Q どうして「ありがとう」じゃなくて「すみません」と言うの？
Why do you say "すみません" instead of "ありがとう"?

A これは迷惑をかけてあやまっているわけじゃなくて、何かしてもらったことに対して「私のために時間と労力を使ってくれてありがとう」というお礼の気持ちを表す言葉になるんだ。「すみません、ありがとうございます」と一緒に言うことも多いよ。

You're not apologizing for causing a nuisance, it's an expression of gratitude for what they've done for you, like saying, "Thank you for spending your time and effort on me." We say "すみません、ありがとうございます" together pretty often, too.

[3] 何かお願いするとき When asking for something  [No.29]

「**すみません**、駅はどこにありますか。」
"Excuse me, where is the station?"

Q いつ使う?
When do you use it?

A 人に何かお願いをするときや、話しかけるときに使うよ。
You use it when asking people for something or when you start to talk to them.

Q どこで使うことが多い?
Where do you use it often?

A お店で注文をするときに、よく使うと思うよ。「すみません、ビールください!」とかね。
You'll use it a lot when ordering at a restaurant. "すみません, beer, please!"

Q まだ何も悪いことをしていないのに、どうして話しかける前に「すみません」と言うの?
Why do you say "すみません" before talking to someone when you haven't done anything wrong yet?

A 「すみません」という言葉は、「これからあなたに話しかけますよ」と知らせるために、必要な言葉なんだ。例えば、知らない人に「駅はどっちですか?!」と急に話しかけられたらびっくりするよね。

The word "すみません" is necessary to let them know that "I'm going to talk to you now." For example, you'd be surprised if someone you don't know suddenly asks, "Where's the station?!"

すみません、注文お願いします!
Excuse me, can I order?

はい!今行きます!
Sure! I'm coming!

意味がいっぱいある言葉 | Words with Lots of Meanings

まとめ

「すみません」を使う場面は3つあるよ！

There are three situations when you use "すみません"!

[1] ごめんなさいとあやまるときの「すみません」
　　"すみません" when saying an apology

[2] ありがとうとお礼を言うときの「すみません」
　　"すみません" when expressing gratitude

[3] 人にお願いごとをする、話しかける前の「すみません」
　　"すみません" when asking for something or before talking to someone

例文で確認！

[1] まだ？もう出発するよ！—— すみません！すぐ行きます。
　　You're still not ready? We're leaving already! —— Sorry! I'll be right there.

[2] 荷物持とうか？—— すみません。お願いします。
　　Shall I carry your luggage? —— Thank you, please.

[3] すみません。もしかして…ゆか先生ですか？—— はい！そうですよ。
　　Excuse me. Could it be... you're Yuka-sensei? —— Yes! That's right.

日本の電車

日本で生活するときは、電車に乗ることが多いと思います。注意しなければいけないのは、日本の電車はとても静かだということです。みんなあまり話をしないんです。大きな声で話すと、みんな嫌な気持ちになってしまいます。だから話をするとしても、周りの人の迷惑にならないように小さな声で話しますよ。私はいつも外国から帰ってきたときに、まずこの電車の静かさに驚きます！あんなにたくさん人がいるのにあんなに静かな場所、他にはあまりないですよね。

Japanese trains

I think people take the train a lot when living in Japan. What you need to take note of is that it's very quiet on Japanese trains. Nobody talks all that much. If you talk loudly, it'll make everyone else feel uncomfortable. That's why even if people talk, they'll speak in a soft voice so they won't bother other people. Whenever I come back from abroad, I'm always first surprised at how quiet the trains are! There aren't many other places that are so quiet even with so many people.

教科書と意味が違う言葉

― Words with Different Textbook Definitions ―

全然
ぜんぜん

Not 〜 at all / Totally

● 教科書の意味 Textbook Definition

「全然〜ない」という形で使います。「全然おいしくない」とか「全然わからない」と言ったら、「少しもおいしくない」「少しもわからない」という意味になります。

It's used in the form of "not 〜 at all." When you say "全然おいしくない" or "全然わからない", it means "it's not delicious at all" or "I don't understand at all."

● 会話での意味 Meaning in Conversation  [No.30]

例文 Example sentence

「ゆかって英語できる？この文章の意味がわからなくて…。」
「**全然**できるよ。みせて！」

"Can you speak English, Yuka? I don't get the meaning of this sentence …"
"I can totally speak it. Let me see!"

Q 教科書と意味が違うことがあるの？
Are there times when it means something different from the textbook?

A うん。もちろん教科書に書かれているように「全然〜ない」と使うこともあるよ。でも、会話の中では後ろに「ない」がつかないこともよくあるんだ。

Yeah. Of course, it's often used as "全然〜ない" like written in the textbook. But in conversations, there are often time you won't put "ない" at the end.

Q 例えば？ For example?

A 「全然おいしい」とか「全然わかる」とかが多いかな。

I think phrases like "全然おいしい" and "全然わかる" are pretty common.

教科書と意味が違う言葉 | Words with Different Textbook Definitions

Q どんな意味？ What does it mean?

A 意味が2つあるよ。1つ目は「とても」の意味。「全然おいしい」は「とてもおいしい」だし、「全然わかる」は「よくわかる」という意味になるんだ。

There are two meanings. First, it can mean "very/totally." "全然おいしい" means "it's very delicious," and "全然わかる" means "I totally get it."

Q 2つ目の意味は？ What's the second meaning?

A 「意外と」という意味もあるよ。It can also mean "unexpectedly."

Q 例えば？ For example?

A 「あんまりおいしくないよ」と言われて食べた料理が、思ったよりまずくはなかったときに「全然おいしいよ」と言うことがあるよ。これは「すごくおいしい」というより「思っていたよりおいしい」という意味になるんだ。

When you eat food that someone said isn't very delicious and it wasn't as bad as you expected, sometimes you'll say, "全然おいしいよ." This means "it's more delicious than I expected" rather than "very delicious."

Q いつ使ってもいいの？ When can you use it?

A 話すときによく使う言葉だから、書くときには使わない方がいいよ。

It's a word used a lot when speaking, so you shouldn't use it when you write.

まとめ 「全然」の教科書にはない使い方
Uses of "全然" not found in textbooks

● **教科書** Textbook

表現方法：**全然** ＋ 否定表現
意　　味：全然〜ない

Expression : 全然 + Negative expression
Meaning : Not 〜 at all

● **会話** Conversation

表現方法：**全然** ＋ 肯定表現
意　　味：① とても〜だ
　　　　　② 意外と〜だ

Expression : 全然 + Positive expression
Meaning : ① Very/Totally 〜
　　　　　② Surprisingly 〜

まあまあ
So-so

教科書の意味 Textbook Definition

「十分じゃないけど、満足できる」という意味です。よくも悪くもないと言いたいときに使います。「ご飯おいしい？」と聞かれて「まあまあ」と答えたら、「おいしくもないし、まずくもない」という意味になります。あまりよくないと思ったときに使います。

It means "not enough, but satisfactory." You use it when you want to say that something is neither good nor bad. If you respond "まあまあ" when asked if your food is good, it means "it's not delicious but it's not bad." You use it when you think something's not so good.

会話での意味 Meaning in Conversation

例文 Example sentence

「あー、おなかすいた。」

「ご飯作ってあげようか？私の料理、**まあまあ**おいしいよ！」

"Ah, I'm hungry."
"Shall I make something for you? My food is pretty good!"

Q 教科書と意味が違うことがあるの？
Are there times when it means something different from the textbook?

A 教科書通り「よくも悪くもない」という意味で使うことが多いよ。でも「まあまあ」の程度は言う人や場面によって高くなることがあるんだ。

It's often used to mean "neither good nor bad" like the textbooks say. But the degree of "まあまあ" can be higher depending on the person who says it and the situation.

教科書と意味が違う言葉 | Words with Different Textbook Definitions

Q 程度が高くなるのは、どんな言い方のとき？
What kind of phrases would make the degree higher?

A 例えば、「日本語を教えてあげようか？ 私、まあまあ得意だよ」と言ったら「上手だ」「よくできる」という意味になるよ。自分で自分のことをほめると変だから「まあまあ」という言葉を使うんだ。

For example, if you say, "Shall I teach you some Japanese? 私、まあまあ得意だよ" it means "I'm skilled at it" or "I can speak it well." It's weird to praise yourself, so you use the word "まあまあ."

Q いつ使う？
When do you use it?

A 友だちとの会話に多いかな。先輩や上司と話すときは使わない方がいいよ。

It's used pretty often when talking with friends. You shouldn't use it when talking to your seniors or boss.

まとめ 「まあまあ」の教科書にはない使い方

Uses of "まあまあ" not found in textbooks

● 教科書 Textbook

表現方法：**まあまあ**
意　　味：よくも悪くもない

Expression : まあまあ
Meaning : Neither good nor bad

● 会話 Conversation

表現方法：**まあまあ**
意　　味：とても〜だ

※特に友だちとの会話でよく使う言い方。
　先生や上司には使わない方がいい。

Expression : まあまあ
Meaning : Pretty / Very 〜

※A phrase often used in conversation, especially with friends. It's better not to use it with teachers and bosses.

おかげで
Thanks to / Because of

● 教科書の意味 Textbook Definition

「先生のおかげで試験に合格できました」のように、「〜がいてくれたから、〜の協力があったからいい結果になりました」とお礼を伝えるときに使う言葉です。いい結果になった原因を表すときに使います。

It's a word used to convey thanks, as in "Thanks to you, Sensei, I was able to pass the exam," meaning "I got good results because of 〜's cooperation / because 〜 was here for me." It's used to indicate the cause of positive results.

● 会話での意味 Meaning in Conversation

例文 Example sentence

「どうしたの？今日は眠そうだね。」
「宿題の**おかげで**、全然眠れなかったよ。」

"What's wrong? You look sleepy today."
"I couldn't sleep at all because of my homework."

Q 教科書と意味が違うことがあるの？
Are there times when it means something different from the textbook?

A うん。悪い結果になった原因を言いたいときに使うこともあるよ。
Yeah. Sometimes it's also used when you want to say the cause of a negative result.

Q 「せい」と同じ意味？ So the same meaning as "せい (because of)"?

A 正解！「おかげ」はいい結果の原因、「せい」は悪い結果の原因を表す文法だと勉強したよね。でも実は「おかげ」も「せい」の意味で使うことがあるんだ。
That's right! You learned the grammar that says "おかげ" expresses the cause of positive results and "せい" is for the cause of negative results. But actually, "おかげ" is sometimes also used to mean "せい."

教科書と意味が違う言葉 | Words with Different Textbook Definitions

Q 例えば？ For example?

A 「先生のおかげで試験に落ちました」と言ったら「先生のせいで試験に落ちた」という意味になるよ。

When you say "I failed the exam thanks to my teacher," it means "I failed the exam because of my teacher."

Q どうして「せい」じゃなくて「おかげ」を使うの？

Why do you use "おかげ" instead of "せい"?

A 「おかげ」を使った方が「先生の教え方が悪かった」「先生に責任がある」と、より相手に原因があることを強く言えるんだ。つまり「皮肉」になる。すごく嫌な言い方だよ。

Using "おかげ" more strongly expresses that the other person is the cause, meaning that "the teacher's teaching methods were bad" or "the teacher was responsible." In other words, it's used ironically. It's a very unpleasant way of saying it.

まとめ 「おかげ」の教科書にはない使い方

Uses of "おかげ" not found in textbooks

● **教科書** Textbook

表現方法：**おかげ＋いい結果**

意　　味：いい結果の原因について、お礼の気持ちを表す

Expression : おかげ + good results
Meaning : Expresses feelings of thanks for causing positive results

● **会話** Conversation

表現方法：**おかげ＋悪い結果**

意　　味：「せい」と同じ意味。悪い結果の原因について、相手を責める気持ちを強く表す

Expression : おかげ + bad results
Meaning : Same meaning as "せい." Express feelings of blame toward the other person for causing negative results

日本の給食
にほん きゅうしょく

日本の小学校・中学校には「給食」というものがあります。全ての学校ではありませんが、お昼ご飯は学校が用意してくれる場合が多いです。私はこの給食が本当に大好きでした！ メニューは毎日変わりますが、私は特にカレーが大好きでした！ ちなみに飲み物はいつも牛乳です。私のクラスでは、いつも余ったデザートをみんなでじゃんけんして取り合っていました。いつも栄養バランスが考えられた、健康的なメニューになっています。ちなみに、料理をお皿に入れたり、席に配ったりするのは生徒の仕事なんですよ。

Japanese school lunch

At elementary and junior high schools in Japan, it's common to have school lunches provided by the school. I really loved these school lunches! The menu would change every day and the curry lunch was my favorite! By the way, the drink we'd get is always milk. In my class, everyone would also fight over the left over dessert by playing rock-paper-scissors. The school lunches always have a healthy menu that considers nutritional balance. By the way, it's the students' job to serve the food onto plates and hand them out to everyone at their seats.

違いがややこしい言葉
― Words with Tricky Differences ―

する予定 & するつもり
Plan to & Intend to

これから行うことを表す表現です。どちらも意味は同じですが、印象が少し違います。
Expressions that show what you're about to do. They both have the same meaning, but give slightly different impressions.

例文 Example sentence [No.33]

「今日の**予定**は？」
「1日中日本語の勉強を**するつもり**だよ。」
"What are your plans today?"
"I'm going to study Japanese all day long."

● 〜する予定 Plan to 〜

Q どんな印象？ What kind of impression does it give?

A いつするのか、どうやってするのかまでくわしく決まっている印象があるよ。
It gives the impression that details like when and how you'll do something have been decided.

Q どうして？ How come?

A 「予定」という言葉は、もうすでにすると決まっていることに使うんだ。
The word "予定" is used for things that have already been decided.

Q 自分がしたいことを言いたいときに使うの？
So you use it when you want to say something you want to do?

A そうだね。他にも、「来年、卒業する予定です」というように、自分がしたいこと以外にも「予定」という言葉を使うことができるんだ。
That's right. You can also use the word "予定" for things other than what you want to do, like "I'm planning to graduate next year."

違いがややこしい言葉 | Words with Tricky Differences

● 〜するつもり　Intend to 〜

Q どんな印象？　What kind of impression does it give?

A 自分の気持ちを強く伝えている印象があるよ。
The impression is that you're strongly conveying your feelings.

Q 気持ち…？　Feelings…?

A だれにも言っていないけど自分の心の中で決めている予定とか、しようと思っていることかな。
Like for plans you haven't told anyone but have decided in your head, or are thinking of doing.

まとめ 「予定&つもり」の違いはこれだ！
The difference between "予定&つもり" is this!

● **予定**　すでにすると決まっている未来のこと ＝ 確定していること
Plan　Things in the future that have already been decided. = Confirmed

● **つもり**　自分がしようと思っている未来のこと ＝ 自分の意思
Intend　Things you're thinking of doing in the future. = Your intention

※印象が変わるだけで、意味は同じ
※They mean the same thing, only the impression changes

例文で確認！

［1］留学する予定 :「もう行く日も行く場所も決まっている」という印象
Gives an impression that the dates and places have already been decided

［2］留学するつもり:「心の中で決心しているけど、
　　　　　　　　　　まだ何も決めていない」という印象
Gives an impression that you're determined to do it in your mind, but haven't decided anything yet

〜でいいです & 〜がいいです
〜 is fine & 〜 is good

日本語は特に、助詞の使い方が難しいです。この2つの言い方、助詞が違うだけなのに、すごく印象が変わります。この違い、わかりますか？

Particles are particularly hard to use in Japanese. Even though just the particles are different for these two phrases, the impression changes a lot. Do you understand this difference?

例文 Example sentence 🔊 [No.34]

「すみません。赤色は売り切れです。」
「そうですか。じゃあ青色でいいです。」

"I'm sorry. Red is sold out."
"Is that so? Blue is fine then."

● 〜でいいです 〜 is fine

Q どんな印象？ What kind of impression does it give?

A 例えば、「それでいいです」だと「満足していないけどそれでいいよ。仕方がないなぁ」という意味だよ。

For example, "それでいいです" means "I'm not satisfied, but that's fine." It can't be helped."

● 〜がいいです 〜 is good

Q どんな印象？ What kind of impression does it give?

A 例えば、「それがいいです」というのは「好きだから、それがいい！」という意味になるんだ。

For example, "それがいいです" means "I like it, so that's good!"

違いがややこしい言葉 | Words with Tricky Differences

Q 日本人でも間違えることはある？

Do Japanese people even mistake them sometimes?

A 私のお父さんとお母さんは、よくこの言い方でけんかしていたなぁ。「今日のご飯は何がいい？」ってお母さんが聞いたときに、お父さんが「あぁ、カレーでいいよ」と言ったら、もうけんかが始まっちゃう！こういうときは「カレーがいいな」と言うのが正解だね。

My mom and dad used to bicker a lot over these phrases. When my mom would ask, "What do you want to eat today?" and my dad said, "あぁ、カレーでいいよ" the bickering would start already! In times like these, the right way answer is to say, "カレーがいいな"

まとめ 「〜でいいです＆〜がいいです」の違いはこれだ！

The difference between "〜でいいです＆〜がいいです" is this!

● 〜でいいです

（あまり好きではないけど、仕方がない）それでいいです。

〜 is fine (I don't really like it, but it can't be helped.)

● 〜がいいです

（好きだから）それがいいです。

〜 is good (because I like it).

※込められている気持ちが全然違うから、使い間違えると相手を怒らせてしまうこともある。
※The feelings in each of them are completely different, so if you use them incorrectly, you might upset the other person.

こういう＆そういう＆ああいう
Like this & Like that & Like that (over there)

これ、それ、あれ、が変化した形で、「こういう・そういう・ああいう」とか「こうやって・そうやって・ああやって」とか「このように・そのように・あのように」とか、いろんな指示語がありますよね。この使い分け、わかりますか？

There are lots of different demonstrative words formed by changing "これ, それ, and あれ" like "こうやって・そうやって・ああやって" and "このように・そのように・あのように", etc. Do you know how to use them properly?

例文 Example sentence [No.35]

「彼女とけんかしたんだ。**こういう**とき、どうすればいいの？」
「**そういう**ときは、ちゃんと話し合った方がいいと思うよ。」

"I fought with my girlfriend. What should I do at a time like this?"
"In times like that, I think it's better to talk it out properly."

まず復習！

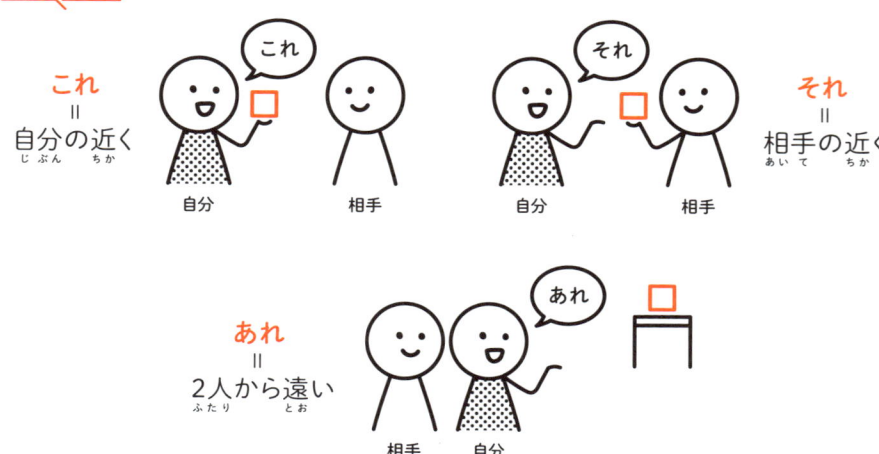

違いがややこしい言葉 | Words with Tricky Differences

● こういう Like this

Q: いつ使う？ When do you use it?

A: 自分が言ったこと・したことについて言いたいときに使うよ！
You it when you want to talk about something you yourself said or did!

Q: 例えば？ For example?

A: 「今日はとても疲れました。こういうときはビールが飲みたくなります。」

これは、自分の話をしているよね。自分がすることについて話しているから「こういう」を使っているんだ。「こういう」を使う場面では、「そういう」を使えることが多いから、この文でも「そういうとき」と言うこともできるよ。

"I'm so exhausted today. At times like this, I want to have a beer."
This is talking about yourself, right? You use "こういう (like this)" because you're talking about what you do. You can use "そういう" in a lot of the situations where you'd use "こういう," so you can also say "そういうとき" in this sentence.

● そういう Like that

Q: いつ使う？ When do you use it?

A: 相手が言ったこと・したことについて言いたいときに使うよ！
Use it when you want to say what the other person said or did!

Q: 例えば？ For example?

A: 「今日はゆかちゃんが大好きなハンバーグを作ったよ。」
「ありがとう。あなたのそういうやさしいところが大好きだよ。」

これは、相手がしてくれたことを伝えているよね。自分じゃなくて、相手について話したいから、「こういう」じゃなくて「そういう」を使っているんだ。

"I made your favorite hamburgers today, Yuka-chan."
"Thanks. I love that sort of kindness of yours."
This conveys you what the other person did for you. You use "そういう (that sort)" instead of "こういう (this sort)" because you want to talk about the other person, not yourself.

● ああいう Like that (over there)

Q いつ使う？ When do you use it?

A 自分からも相手からも遠いものについて言いたいときに使うよ！
You use it when you want to talk about something that's far away from you and the other person!

Q 例えば？ For example?

A 「ゆか先生、やさしくてきれいだな〜。」
「そうだよね。ああいう人になりたいよ。」
これは、この場所にいない人について話しているよね。つまり、会話をしている2人から遠い人だから、ここでは「こういう人」「そういう人」ではなくて「ああいう人」と言っているんだよ。

"Yuka-sensei is so kind and beautiful."
"You're right. I want to be that kind of person."
In this case, they're talking about someone who isn't at that place. In other words, because it's someone that's far away from the 2 people having a conversation, they wouldn't say "こういう人" or "そういう人" here, but "ああいう人".

まとめ 「こういう & そういう & ああいう」の違いはこれだ！
The difference between "こういう & そういう & ああいう" is this!

- **こういう** 自分が言ったこと・したことについて言いたいとき
  When you want to talk about something you said or did

- **そういう** 相手が言ったこと・したことについて言いたいとき
  When you want to talk about something the other person said or did

- **ああいう** 自分からも相手からも遠いものについて言いたいとき
  When you want to talk about something that's far away from both you and the other person

意味がややこしい言い方

― Words with Complicated Meanings ―

「明日まで」って、いつまで?

Until when is "明日まで"?

例文 Example sentence [No.36]

「明日までにこの資料まとめといて。」
「すみません、明日の何時まででしょうか?」

"Put these materials together by tomorrow."
"I'm sorry, by what time tomorrow?"

Q 「明日まで」はいつまで?
Until when is "明日まで"?

A 「明日(が終わる)まで」という意味だから、「明日の23:59まで」だよ。
It means "by (the end of) tomorrow," so it means "by 23:59 tomorrow."

Q でも、そうじゃないこともありますよね…?
But sometimes that's not the case, right…?

A そうなんだよね。「明日まで」がいつまでかは「場合によって変わる」んだよ。
That's right. The timing of "明日まで" will change depending on the situation.

Q 例えば?
For example?

A 会社で「明日までに提出して」と言われたら、「明日の朝1番に提出する」かもしれないし、「仕事が終わる5時まで」かもしれない。それは、相手に確認しないとはっきりわからないんだ。

If someone at work says "明日までに提出して" it may mean "have it in first thing tomorrow morning," or "by the time work finishes at 5 o'clock." You can't tell without checking with the other person.

まとめ

「明日までに」は、明日が終わるまで！でも…

"明日までに" means by the end of tomorrow! But...

明日まで＝明日の23:59まで
3月30日まで＝3月30日の23:59まで

※ 会社の場合は、「営業時間が終わるまで」という意味になることが多い。
※ 相手が何月何日の何時までだと思っているのかを確認した方がいい。

明日まで = by 23:59 tomorrow
3月30日まで = By 23:59 on March 30th

※ The workplace, it often means "by the end of business hours."
※ You should check what month, date, and time the other person is thinking of.

JLPTの申し込み、**明日まで**らしいよ！
It seems like JLPT applications are until tomorrow!

明日の何時までなんだろう…？
I wonder until what time tomorrow...?

「前のページ」って、先？後ろ？

What is "前のページ"? The next page? The previous one?

例文 Example sentence 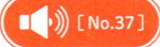 [No.37]

「みなさん、ひとつ前のページを開いてください。」

「前…？」

"Everyone, please open up the previous page."
"Previous...?"

Q 「前のページに書いてあるよ」って言われたら、ページを進める？ それとも戻るの？

If you are told "前のページに書いてあるよ," do you move on to the next page? Or go back to the last one?

A 正解は「戻る」！

The correct answer is go back to the last one!

Q 「未来＝前」、「過去＝後ろ」じゃないの？

Doesn't "future = 前" and "past = 後ろ"?

A 場所について話すときに「前」と言ったら、自分がいる場所よりも進んだ場所を表すよね。
でも時間や物事の流れをについて話すときに「前」と言ったら、過去を表す言葉になるんだ。

If you say "前" when talking about a place, it means a place that is ahead of where you are then. But when you say "前" talking about the flow time and things, it turns into a word describing the past.

場所の「前」　　　　時間の「前」

意味がややこしい言い方 | Words with Complicated Differences

Q 例えば？

For example?

A 「あの店には、前行ったことがある」「ゆかさんは前のリーダーだ」、こういう文では、「過去」の意味で使われるんだ。でも、「前の席にゆかさんがいる」「前に進む」、こういう文では「未来」とか「先」という意味になるよ。

"I've been to that store before," or "Yuka-san was the previous leader." In these kind of sentences, it's used to mean the past. But in sentences like "Yuka-san is in the front seat," or "Move forward," it means "future" or "ahead."

「先」は、ものの前のことだよね。
でも「先日」と言ったら、
「過去」を表す言葉になるんだよ。

"先" means ahead of something, right?
But when you say "先日,"
it's referring to the past.

まとめ

「前のページ」と言われたら、1ページ戻る！

If someone says "前のページ," go back 1 page!

日本語の「前」には2つの意味がある。
物理的な場所を表す「前」＝進む
時間的な流れを表す「前」＝戻る、過去

The Japanese word "前" has 2 meanings.
"前" referring to a physical location = move forward
"前" referring to the flow of time = go back, the past

「1日おきに来る」って、いつ来るの？

If someone says "1日おきに来る," when do they come?

例文 Example sentence  [No.38]

「1日おきに彼から連絡がくるんだ。」
「そっか。毎日連絡してほしいよね。」

"He contacts me every other day."
"I see... You'd want him to contact you every day, right?"

Q　「1日おきに来る」っていつ来るの？

　　If someone says "1日おきに来る," when do they come?

A　「1日を間におく」という意味だから、「1日おきに彼が来る」だったら、「彼は今日来て、明日は来ない、次に来るのは明後日」となるよ。

　　It means "to leave 1 day in between", so "1日おきに彼が来る" means "he comes today, tomorrow he doesn't, and next time he'll come is the day after tomorrow."

Q　でも、そうじゃないこともありますよね…？

　　But sometimes that's not the case, right…?

A　うん。言う人の考えや、聞く人の感じ方によっても変わることがあるよ。

　　Yeah. It can change depending on the speaker's intent or how the listener perceives it.

Q　例えば？

　　For example?

A　「3秒おきに電気がつきます」「1年おきに試験を受けます」のように、いろんな単位を使えるよね。教科書の意味通りなら、「6秒に1回電気がつく」「2年に1回試験を受ける」なんだけど、「3秒に1回」「1年に1回」と思ってしまう人もいるんだ。

　　You can use it with various units, like "3秒おきに電気がつきます" or "1年おきに試験を受けます" Going by the textbook definition, these mean "The light turns on once every 6 seconds" and "I take the exam once every two years," but some people think they mean "once every 3 seconds" and "once a year."

意味がややこしい言い方 | Words with Complicated Differences

Q 難しい…。どうしたらいいの？

That's difficult. .. What should I say?

A 「おきに」という言葉の代わりに「ごとに」を使うといいよ！「〜ごとに」は「〜をするときいつもする」という意味だから、「3秒ごとに」は「3秒に1回」、「6秒ごとに」は「6秒に1回」という意味をはっきり表すことができるんだ。

Use "ごとに" instead of the word "おきに"! "〜ごとに" means "you do something every time you 〜," so 3秒ごとに and 6秒ごとに can clearly express that you mean "once every 3 seconds " and "once every 6 seconds."

まとめ

「1日おきに」は、2日に1度！でも…

"1日おきに" is once every two days! But...

○○おきに ＝ ○○を間におく

1日おきに＝1日を間におく ＝ 2日に1度

半年おきに＝半年を間におく ＝ 1年に1度

※「おきに」はいろんな理解の方法があるので、間違いが起きる可能性がある。

※ 代わりに「ごとに」を使えば、もっとはっきり伝えることができる。

○○おきに ＝ Leaving ○○ in between
1日おきに ＝ leaving 1 day in between ＝ once every 2 days
半年おきに ＝ leaving 6 months in between ＝ Once a year

※ There are many different understandings of "おきに," so it's possible mistakes can occur.
※ If you use "ごとに" instead, you can convey what you mean more clearly

「もらってあげてくれる?」って、だれに何をするの?

"もらってあげてくれる?" means doing what for who?

 **Example sentence**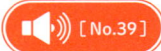

子ども 「これあげる!」

お母さん 「ゆかちゃん、これ**もらってあげてくれる**?」

Child "You can have this!"
Mother "Yuka-chan, could you have that for them?"

Q そもそも「もらってくれる?」も難しい…。「もらってくれる?」はいつ使うの?

"もらってくれる?" is hard in the first place … When do you use "もらってくれる?"

A 例えば、クッキーをたくさん作りすぎて1人で全部食べられないとき、だれかに食べてほしいと思うよね。そのときに「このクッキー、もらってくれない?」と言ってお願いすることがあるよ。

For example, if you've made too many cookies and you can't eat them all by yourself, you'd want someone to eat them, right? At that time, sometimes you might ask "このクッキー、もらってくれない?"

Q じゃあ、「もらってあげてくれる?」ってどんな意味?

Then what does "もらってあげてくれる?" mean?

A 「あなたがこのクッキーを『もらう』ということを、この人のために『してくれませんか』?」というお願いだよ。

It's a request asking if "you can 'have or receive' this cookie 'for him/her'".

Q え…? どんな場面で使うの?

Huh…? In what kind of situation would you use it?

A 例えば、自分の子どもがクッキーをたくさん作って、それを友だちのもりおくんにあげようとしているときに、「もりおくん、クッキーもらってあげてくれる?」と言うんだ。つまり、お母さんが子どもの立場になって話しているんだね。

For example, if a mother's child makes a lot of cookies and they try to give some to his/her friend, Morio-kun, she'd say, "もりおくん、クッキーもらってあげてくれる?" In other words, the mother is talking from her child's standpoint.

意味がややこしい言い方 | Words with Complicated Differences

まとめ

「もらってあげてくれる?」は、お母さんが自分の子どもの代わりにお願いしている!

"もらってあげてくれる?" is the mother making a request in her child's place!

「もらってあげてくれる?」を使うときは3人いる。
「『もらう』ということを『してあげてくれますか』?」と、お母さんが自分の代わりにお願いするときに使う。
親と子どものように、話している3人の中で2人の関係が、もう1人の相手よりも近い場合、この言い方が使える。

There are 3 people involved when you use "もらってあげてくれる?"
It's used when your mother asks, "Can you 'have or receive' something from them 'for me?'" in the child's place.
This phrase can be used when the relationship between 2 of the 3 people speaking is closer than with the other person, like a parent and a child.

お菓子作ったんだけど、あやの先生もらってくれるかな…?
I made some sweets, but I wonder if Ayano-sensei would have some for me…?

あやの先生ー!もりおくんがお菓子作ったんだって。
もらってあげてくれる?

Ayano-sensei! Morio-kun said he made some sweets.
Could you have some of them from him?

わーい!もりおくん、ありがとう!
Wow! Thank you, Morio-kun!

会話 ②-1 「日本語の森」でお仕事中
Working at "Nihongo no Mori"

 [No.40]

> あやの先生、お疲れ様！
> 今日6時から飲み会だけど、**大丈夫だよね**[1]？
>
> Thanks for your hard work, Ayano-sensei!
> There's a drinking party from 6 o'clock today, you're okay to come, right[1]?

> あ、忘れてました！
> **すみません**[2]。まだ残ってる仕事があって…。
>
> Oh, I'd forgotten! I'm sorry[2]. I still have work left...

> そうなんだ。手伝おうか？
>
> Is that so? Shall I help?

> いや、そんな、**いいですよ**[3]。
> 作業いっぱい残ってるんで。
>
> No, it's fine[3]. I have a lot of work left.

> どれ？…この資料作るだけでしょ？
> **全然**[4]余裕じゃん！ すぐやろう！
>
> Which ones? ... just making these materials, right?
> There's plenty of time[4]! Let's do it right away!

> **すみません**[2]。よろしくお願いします！
>
> Sorry to bother you[2]. Thanks for your help!

―――― 作業中 Working ――――

終わったー！飲みに行こう！
All done! Let's go for drinks!

ありがとうございました！
ゆか先生の**おかげ**(5)で早く終わりました。
Thank you! We finished early thanks to you(5), Ms. Yuka.

あやの先生の**おかげ**(6)で、
いっぱい仕事させられたなー。
I got to do lots of work thanks to you(6) Ms. Ayano.

…**すみません**(2)。
…Sorry to bother you(2).

(1)「問題ない」の意味　　Meaning "no problem"
(2)「ごめんなさい」の意味　　Meaning "I'm sorry"
(3)「必要ない」の意味　　Meaning "not necessary"
(4)「とても〜だ」の意味　　Meaning "very much"
(5) いい結果の原因　　The cause of good results
(6) 悪い結果の原因　　The cause of bad results

結婚したい?

Do you want to get married?

 [No.41]

ゆか先生って、結婚したいですか?
Yuka-sensei, do you want to get married?

まあ、いい人がいればって感じかなー。
あやの先生は?
Well, I would, if there was a good person.
What about you, Ayano-sensei?

私は32歳までに結婚する**つもり**⁽¹⁾なんです!
I intend (1) to get married by 32!

そうなんだ!
私、来月友だちの結婚式に参加する**予定**⁽²⁾なんだけど、
多分行ったら結婚したくなっちゃうと思う!
Is that so!
I'm planning (2) to attend my friend's wedding next month,
so I think I'll probably want to get married once I go!

そういうこと⁽³⁾、ありますよね。
It really is like that (3), right?

昔は絶対結婚しない**つもり**(1)だったんだけど、
友だちの結婚式に参加するたびに
「いいなー」って思うようになって。

I was absolutely never(1) going to get married before,
but I've started to feel jealous every time I go to a friend's wedding.

この前の中本先生の結婚式も最高でしたよね。

Nakamoto-sensei's wedding recently was awesome, too.

うんうん！**ああいう場所**(4)で結婚式できたら最高だな〜！

Yeah yeah! It would be amazing to have a wedding in that kind of place(4)!

でも、ゆか先生…まずは恋人見つけないと…。

But Yuka-sensei... you have to find a partner first...

わかってるって、うるさいな！

Of course I know that, you're annoying!

(1) 自分の意思　　　　　　　　　Own intention

(2) 確定していること　　　　　　Confirmed

(3) 相手が言ったこと・したこと　　When you want to talk about something
　　について言いたいとき　　　　the other person said or did

(4) 自分からも相手からも遠いもの　When you want to talk about something that's
　　について言いたいとき　　　　far away from you and the other person

仕事の相談
Work consultation

来週YouTubeにアップする動画、
明日まで(1)に撮影してくれる？

So that video we're going to upload to YouTube next week, can you shoot it for me by tomorrow(1)?

はい！じゃあ、今すぐ撮影してきますね！

Yes! I'll go shoot it right now, then!

いや、そんな急がなくていいよ。
明日まで(1)って言ったけど、
明後日から編集するからそれまでにお願い。

It's fine, you don't have to rush.
I said by tomorrow(1), but I'll edit it from the day after tomorrow, so please get it done by then.

はい！わかりました！

Sure! Got it!

あと、これから**1週間おきに**(2)
動画アップすることにしたから、
撮影忙しくなるけどがんばろうね。

Also, I decided to upload a video every other week(2) from now on so we'll be busy shooting, but let's do our best.

え？大変ですかね？
2週間に1本なら、**全然**(3)できますよ。

Huh? Is that so hard? If it's one video every two weeks, we can totally do it(3).

あ、ごめん、**1週間ごとに**(2)アップするっていう意味。
1週間に1本ね。

Oh, sorry, I mean that we'll upload every week(2). One video a week, yeah?

それはまあまあ大変だな…。

That will be pretty tough...

前の(4)動画見直して、
人気があったシリーズの撮影しよう。

Let's review our previous(4) video
and shoot for the series that were popular.

はい！

Alright!

(1) 明日まで＝明日の23:59まで   By tomorrow = By 23:59 tomorrow
(2) 1週間に1度   Once a week
(3) とても〜だ   Very / Totally 〜
(4) 昔   Previously / before

日本の学校のルール

　日本の学校には「校則」という学校のきまりがあって、それがすごく厳しいんです。特に中学校・高校は校則が厳しい学校が多いです。日本は「みんな同じがいい」という考えがけっこう強いので、生徒たちの見た目や行動がみんな同じになるようにルールが決められているんです。

例えば…
- 制服のスカートの丈は絶対に膝の下までないといけない
- シャツのボタンは1番上までとめないといけない
- かみの色を染めてはいけない
- かみの毛が肩につく長さなら、結ばないといけない
- ピアスやタトゥーは禁止

など

おしゃれしたい…
I want to dress up...

　もちろんすべての学校にこういうルールがあるわけではありません。そして、時代が変化するにつれて少しルールもゆるくなっているようには感じます。でも私が学生のときはこういうルールでした。やばいでしょ？

Japanese school rules

Japanese schools have a set of "school rules" they've decided on that are really strict. There are many junior high schools and high schools in particular with strict rules. In Japan, there's a strong mindset that "everyone should be the same," so rules are set so that all students look and act the same way.

For example...
- Uniform skirts must reach below the knee
- Shirts must be buttoned up to the very top
- Hair cannot be dyed
- Hair long enough to touch the shoulders must be tied up
- Piercings and tattoos are prohibited

etc.

Of course, not all schools have these rules. And I feel that the rules are becoming a bit more lenient as the times change. But when I was a student, these were the rules. Aren't they crazy?

これができたら、会話上級者！

If you can use these, you'll be a conversation expert！

- P.113〜　**便利なあいづち**
  Convenient Aizuchi (Interjections)

- P.125〜　**にごす言葉**
  Vague Words

- P.135〜　**クッション言葉**
  Cushion Words

- P.152〜　**怒るときの言葉**
  Words for when Angry

- P.161〜　**気持ちを表す言葉**
  Words to Express Feelings

3章、はじまるよ！

便利なあいづち

― Convenient Aizuchi (Interjections) ―

※ あいづち：相手の話を聞いているということを
表すための短い言葉

※ Aizuchi (Interjections): Short words to indicate that you're listening to the other person.

なるほど

I see

例文 Example sentence [No.43]

「私のお母さん、チョコレートが大好きだったから、私も好きになったんだ。」
「**なるほど**ね。」

"My mom loved chocolate, so I came to love it too."
"I see."

意味 Meaning

- 相手が言った言葉に対して、「よくわかった」「その通りだ」という気持ちを表すときに使う
- 相手が言って初めて気がついたことがあるときによく使う

- It's used to express the feeling that what the other person said is "well understood" or "that's right."
- You often use it for something you've realized for the first time once the other person said it.

使い方 Usage

[1]「今日、頭が痛くてさ。」
「**なるほど**、だから朝からあんまりしゃべってなかったんだ。」

"I've got a headache today."
"I see, that's why you haven't talked much since this morning."

[2]「『日本語の森』の人気があるのは、いい先生がたくさんいるからなんだって。」
「**なるほど**！」

"I heard the reason why 'Nihongo no Mori' is so popular is because they have a lot of good teachers."
"I see!"

便利なあいづち | Convenient Aizuchi (Interjections)

ポイント Point

「なるほど」という言葉は、「あなたの言っていることは正しい」というように、相手の言ったことを評価している印象を与えることがあります。先生や上司に使うと失礼になる場合がありますよ。使うときは「なるほど！そうなんですね！」や「あぁー！なるほど！知らなかったです！」のように気持ちを込めて言った方がいいです。

The word "なるほど" can give the impression that you're evaluating what the other person's said, like "what you're saying is right." It can be rude if you use it with teachers or bosses. You should say it with feeling when using it, like "なるほど！Is that so!" or "Ah! なるほど！I didn't know that!"

似ているフレーズ Similar Phrases

● **確かに！** Certainly!

相手の意見に対して「私もそう思う！」と強く同意する気持ちを表す。

Expresses strong agreement with the other person's opinion, like "I think so too!"

● **そうですね** That's so

相手の意見に対して、同意する気持ちを表す。軽い同意のときにも使える1番使いやすい言い方。

Expresses agreement with the other person's opinion. It's easiest phrase to use that can also be used to express light agreement.

● **おっしゃる通りです** You are correct

「あなたの言っていることに同意します」という意味。「おっしゃる」は「言う」の尊敬語なので、先生や会社の上司によく使う言い方。

Means "I agree with what you are saying." "おっしゃる" is the respectful form of "言う," so it's often used towards teachers and bosses.

「なるほど！確かにそうですね！おっしゃる通りです。」のように、一緒に使うこともありますよ。

Sometimes they're also used together, as in 「なるほど！確かにそうですね！おっしゃる通りです。」

フレーズ 3-2 いいね
How nice

例文 Example sentence [No.44]

「夏休み、みんなで海に行かない?」
「**いいね!**」

"Why don't we all go to the beach over summer vacation?"
"Nice!"

意味 Meaning

- 言葉の通り「いい」という意味
- 見た目や持ち物など、相手のことについてほめるときや、相手の言っていることに対して自分も賛成する、同意すると言いたいときにも使う

- As the word indicates, it means "good/nice."
- It's also used when you want to compliment the other person for things like their appearance or belongings, or when you want to agree or concur with what the other person is saying.

使い方 Usage

[1]「かみ型変えた?すごく**いいね!**」

"Did you get a new hairstyle? It looks really good!"

[2]「今から飲みに行かない?」
　　「**いいね!**」

"Want to go for a drink now?"
"Sounds good!"

[3]「村上さんのアイデア、すごく**いいですね**。」

"Murakami-san, your idea is really good."

便利なあいづち | Convenient Aizuchi (Interjections)

ポイント Point

相手をほめるときは、「いいね！」だけでも十分です。でも、「いいね、すごく似合ってる」や「その服、色がすごくいいね」のように、具体的にほめることが多いです。ほめられた人は、とてもうれしい気持ちになりますよ。

ちなみに、SNSでよく見る「LIKE」ボタンですが、日本語では「いいね！」と表示されます。「とてもすてきです」「私もそれが好きです」という気持ちを表すボタンですね。そして、「LOVE」は「超いいね！」と表示されますよ。

When complimenting someone, just "いいね！" is enough. But it's common to compliment someone specifically, like "Nice, it looks great on you," or "The colors on those clothes are really nice." The person complimented will feel really delighted.
By the way, the "LIKE" button that you often see on social media is displayed as "いいね！" in Japanese. The button expresses feeling that something's "very nice" or that you also like that. And "LOVE" is displayed as "超いいね！"

似ているフレーズ Similar Phrases

● **いい感じだね** Seems good

「いいね！」と同じ意味です。ただ「いいね！」とはっきりした言葉でストレートに伝えるのがちょっとはずかしいときや、全体的にほめたいときに「感じ」をつけることがよくあります。「かみ型変えた？すごくいい感じだね！」と言ったら、「かみ型がかわいいし、あなたによく似合っている。全体的にすてきだ」というような意味になります。聞いた印象が少し変わるだけなので、どちらを使ってもいいですよ。

Has the same meaning as "いいね！" "感じ" is often added when it's a little embarrassing to say "いいね！" in a straightforward manner, or when complimenting something as a whole. If you were to say, "Did you get a new hairstyle? すごくいい感じだね" it means, "The hairstyle is cute and looks good on you. It's lovely overall." The impression the listener gets only changes a bit, so it doesn't matter which one you use.

いいね！
How nice!

うん！いい感じだね。
Yeah! Seems good.

そうなの?

Is that so?

例文 Example sentence [No.45]

「ゆか先生って、ベトナム語も話せるらしいよ。」
「そうなの?」

"Seems like Yuka-sensei can speak Vietnamese too."
"Is that so?"

意味 Meaning

- 相手が言ったことに対して、驚いた気持ちを表す言葉
- 予想していたことと違ったときや、知らなかったことを教えてもらって驚いたときに使う

- It's a phrase expressing feelings of surprise at what the other person said.
- It's used when something is different from what you expected or when you're surprised to learn something you didn't know.

使い方 Usage

[1]「ゆか先生、来月結婚するらしいよ。」
　　「え!**そうなの?**」

"Seems Yuka-sensei is getting married next month."
"Eh! Is that so?"

[2]「あの人の名前、『とよたさん』じゃなくて『とよださん』だよ。」
　　「**そうなの**? ずっと間違えてた…。」

"That person's name is 'Toyoda-san,' not 'Toyota-san.'"
"Is that so? I've been messing it up this whole time…"

便利なあいづち | Convenient Aizuchi (Interjections)

ポイント Point

「そうなの？」と言うときは、びっくりした顔をしながら「の」を上げて言うと気持ちが伝わりやすいです。「そうなの…」と静かに言うと、びっくりしているというより、相手の言ったことで悲しい気持ちになっている言い方になります。

It's easier to convey your feelings when you say "そうなの？" by raising your voice for the "の" while making a surprised face. If you say "そうなの…" quietly, it's more as though you're sad because of what the other person has said rather than surprised.

似ているフレーズ Similar Phrases

● **本当に？** Really?

「そうなの？」と同じ意味です。本当かどうか信じられないというよりも、信じられないと思うほどびっくりしている、という気持ちを表すことができます。

It has the same meaning as "そうなの？" It can express feelings incredible surprise, rather than disbelief at whether or not what's been said is true.

● **まじで？／がちで？** Seriously? / Really?

これはスラングなので、仲のいい友だち同士でしか使うことができません。「本当に？」と同じ意味で使うことができますよ。「まじ」は「真面目」からきている言葉だと言われていて、「がち」は「本気で取り組む」ことを表す「がちんこ」を短く言った言葉だと言われています。どちらも「本気、真剣」と言う意味があるんですね。

These are slang, so they can only be used among close friends. They can be used with the same meaning as "本当に？" "まじ" is said to come from "真面目 (serious)," and "がち" is said to be a shortened form of "がちんこ," which means "to work on something seriously." Both share the meaning of "seriously, earnestly."

うーん
Umm

例文 Example sentence 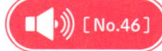 [No.46]

「明日、朝の6時に公園集合ね！」
「うーん…9時にしない？6時は早すぎるよ。」

"Let's meet at the park at 6 tomorrow morning!"
"Uhh... can we make it 9? 6 o'clock is too early."

意味 Meaning

- 相手の言ったことに対して反対の意見があるときや、あまり理解していないときに使う
- 何も話さないと相手が不安になるので、「返事を今、考えています」という気持ちを表したいときにも使う

- You use this when you disagree with what the other person said, or when you don't understand something well.
- You can express that "I'm thinking about my response now," because if you don't say anything, it'll make the other person nervous.

使い方 Usage

[1]「この服どう？似合う？」
　　「うーん…まあまあかな。」

"How's this outfit? Does it look good on me?"
"Umm... it's so-so, I guess."

[2]「この問題、わかった？」
　　「うーん。」

"Did you understand this problem?"
"Umm... "

便利なあいづち | Convenient Aizuchi (Interjections)

ポイント Point

「うーん」と言いながら悩んでいる顔をすると、気持ちがよく伝わります。
If you make a worried face while saying "うーん" it'll convey your feelings better.

似ているフレーズ Similar Phrases

● ええ… Eh...

意味は同じですが、反対意見や不満があるという気持ちがもっとよく伝わります。
It means the same thing, but this better conveys feelings of disagreement and dissatisfaction.

● いやぁ… Nah...

意味は同じですが、反対意見や不満があるという気持ちがもっとよく伝わります。
It means the same thing, but this better conveys feelings of disagreement and dissatisfaction.

このケーキ、食べていい？
Can I eat this cake?

うーん…。
Umm…

121

へぇー
Really?

例文 Example sentence  [No.47]

「昨日、ゆか先生に会ったよ。」
「へぇー！」

"I saw Yuka-sensei yesterday."
"Really?"

意味 Meaning

- 相手の話を「聞いているよ」と伝えることができる言葉
- 相手が言ったことに対して、少し驚いた気持ちを表す言葉
- そんなに驚く話じゃなくても、自分が初めて聞いた話であれば使うことができる
- 気持ちを表すというより、「聞いています、あなたの話を理解しています」ということを伝えることができる

- It's a phrase can convey that you're listening to the other person's story.
- The phrase expresses a bit of surprise at what the other person said.
- Even if it's not something that's so surprising, you can use it if it's the first time you've heard it.
- It allows you to convey that "I'm listening, I understand what you're saying" more so than to express your feelings.

使い方 Usage

[1]「明日から旅行に行くんだ！」
　「へぇー、いいなぁ。」

　"I'm going on a trip tomorrow!"
　"Really, that's so nice."

[2]「あの2人、付き合ってるらしいよ。」
　「へぇー、そうなんだ。」

　"Seems like those two are dating."
　"Really, is that so?"

便利なあいづち | Convenient Aizuchi (Interjections)

ポイント Point

「へぇー」という言葉は、首をたてにふりながら気持ちを込めて言いましょう。小さな声で気持ちを込めずに「へぇー」と言うと、「あなたの話にもう飽きました」「面白くない」と聞こえます。「へぇー」ばかり使っていると、「ちゃんと話を聞いていない」と相手が思うので注意しましょう。

Say the word "へぇー" with feeling while nodding your head. If you say "へぇー" in a quiet voice without any emotion, it'll be taken as "I'm tired of your story" or "This isn't interesting." Be careful not to only ever use "へぇー," because the other person will think you're not listening properly.

似ているフレーズ Similar Phrases

● **ふーん** Hmm

ほとんど同じ意味ですが、「へぇー」よりも、興味がない感じに聞こえる可能性が高い言葉です。言い方に注意しましょう。

It has almost the same meaning, but it's more likely that you'll come across as uninterested rather than with "へぇー." Be careful with how you say it

● **そっかー** Right / Uh-huh

相手の話をわかっているということを、伝えたいときに使います。

Used when you want to convey that you understand what the other person is talking about.

便利なあいづち「さしすせそ」

「さすが！」「しらなかった！」「すごい！」「センスいい！」「そうなんだ！」
相手にいい印象をもってもらうためのあいづち「さしすせそ」と言われています。

[さ] もう仕事おわったよ。── さすが部長！　早いですね！（ほめる）

[し] この道通ると、早く行けるよ。── へー！　知らなかったです！（驚く）

[す] N1 合格したよ。── すごい！（ほめる）

[せ] この服、新しいんだけど、どうかな？── センスいいですね〜！（持ち物をほめる）

[そ] 今日、ゆか先生の誕生日なんだって。── そうなんだ！（驚く）

すごく便利でしょ？　ぜひ使ってみてくださいね！

The 5 convenient "さしすせそ" interjections

"さすが！(As expected!)" "しらなかった！(I didn't know that!)" "すごい！(Wow!)" "センスいい！(Nice taste!)" "そうなんだ！(Is that right!)"
These aizuchi (interjections) used to give the other person a good impression are called the "さしすせそ" aizuchi.

I've finished work already. ── "さすが, director! You finished so early! (Praise)
If you take this road, you'll get there faster. ── Huh! I しらなかったです！(Surprise)
I passed N1. ── すごい！" (Praise)
This outfit is new, but I wonder how it looks? ── センスいいですね！(Praise for belongings)
Today's Yuka-sensei's birthday. ── そうなんだ！(Surprise)

They're very handy, aren't they? Be sure to try using them!

にごす言葉
― Vague Words ―

※にごす言葉:相手に自分の意見をやさしく伝えるための、はっきりしない言葉
※Vague words: Words used to gently convey your opinion to the other person that are unclear

なんか
Like

例文 Example sentence  [No.48]

「昨日、ゆか先生に会ったんでしょ？」
「うん。でも**なんか**、あまり元気そうじゃなかったな。」

"You saw Yuka-sensei yesterday, right?"
"Yeah. But like, she didn't look very well."

意味 Meaning

- 「何か」の音が変化してできた言葉
- 「なんか食べたい」のように「何か」の意味で使うことや、「なんか頭が痛い」のように「どうしてかわからないけど」という意味で使うことがある
- 会話では、はっきりした意味もなく使うことが多い

- This word is a sound change of "何か."
- It's often used to mean "something," as in "I want to eat something," or to mean "I'm not sure why," as in "my head, like, hurts for some reason."
- In conversation, it's often used without any clear meaning.

使い方 Usage

[1]「**なんか**さー、昨日、友だちとご飯食べに行ったんだけどさ、**なんか**すごい人が多くて、疲れたから何も食べずにすぐ帰ったんだ。」

"So like, I went out to eat with my friends yesterday, but there were like, so many people that it tired me out and I went home right away without having anything."

[2]「新しい映画、もう見た？」
「見たよ！でも**なんか**、話が難しくて面白くなかったな。」

"Have you seen that new movie?"
"I saw it! But like, the story was hard to follow and not very interesting."

にごす言葉 | Vague Words

〜っていうか

I mean / By the way

例文 Example sentence [No.49]

「今日、疲れてるね。」
「うん。疲れてる**っていうか**、すごく眠いんだよね。」

"You're so tired today."
"Yeah. It's not that I'm tired, I'm just really sleepy."

意味 Meaning

- 「〜というか」を会話で使うときの言い方
- 「〜というよりもっとぴったりな言い方がある」と言いたいときに使う言葉
- 「っていうか」と会話の中で使う場合は、自分の気持ちや意見をはっきり言いたくないときに使うことが多い
- 会話の最初につけて「ところで」と話を変える使い方もある

- A way to say "〜というか" when used in conversation
- It's a phrase used when you want to say "there's a more perfect way to say it than 〜."
- In conversation, it's often uses when you don't want to express your feelings or opinions clearly.
- It can also be placed at the beginning of a conversation meaning "by the way" to change the topic.

使い方 Usage

[1] 「田中くんのこと、好きなの？」
　　「いや、まぁ、**好きっていうか**、ちょっと気になるだけ。」

"Do you like Tanaka-kun?"
"No, well, I mean I don't like him, I'm just interested."

[2] 「昨日のドラマ、見た？最高だったよね？」
　　「見た見た！めっちゃ面白かったなー！あれ、**っていうか**、かみの毛切った？」

"Did you watch the show yesterday? It was awesome, right?"
"Yeah, I saw it! It was so interesting! Wait, by the way, did cut your hair?"

〜みたいな

〜Like

例文 Example sentence [No.50]

「その服、すごく似合ってるよ。買えば？」
「うん。でも、ちょっと高いかな？**みたいな**。かわいいけど…どうしよう！」

"That outfit looks great on you. What if you bought it?"
"Yeah. But I feel it's like, a bit expensive. It's cute, though...what should I do!"

意味 Meaning

- 自分の気持ちや考えをはっきり伝えたくないときや、はっきり伝えるのがはずかしいときによく使う
- 「〜みたいな感じ」と言って、もっとはっきりしない言い方をする場合も多い
- 「発話文」+「みたいな」と言った場合は、そのような気持ちになった、という意味にもなる

- It's often used when you don't want to express your thoughts and feelings clearly, or when it's embarrassing to.
- In many cases, "〜みたいな感じ (〜like feeling)" is used to say something even more unclearly.
- When you say a sentence + "みたいな," it can also means that you felt that way.

使い方 Usage

[1]「え、プレゼント？ありがとう！でも、どうして？今日、誕生日じゃないよ？」
　　「え、なんか、かわいい服を見つけたから。よろこぶかな、**みたいな**。」

"Huh, a present? Thanks! But why? Today isn't my birthday."
"Oh, like, 'cause I found some cute clothes. I thought, like, it'd make you happy."

[2]「最初は彼のこと嫌いだったんだけど、話してみるとけっこう面白くて、気がついたら好きかも？**みたいな感じ**になってたんだよね。」

"I didn't like him at first, but once I talked to him, he was pretty interesting, and by the time I realized I felt like I might like him?"

にごす言葉 | Vague Words

まあ
well

例文 Example sentence [No.51]

「スマホがなくなっちゃった。**まあ**、いいか。」

「よくないでしょ！早く探しに行こう！」

"I lost my phone. Well, whatever."
"It's not whatever! Let's go find it quick!"

意味 Meaning

- 話し始める前につけて、会話を少しやわらかくするために使う
- 「まあ」はいろんな意味がある
- 「まあいいか」のように、「十分じゃないけど我慢できる」と言いたいときや、「まあ試してみよう」のように、「うまくいかないと思うけどやってみよう」と思うときなど、いろんな場面で使う
- 会話では、特に意味もなく使うことがある

- Placed before you start talking, it's used to make the conversation sound a bit softer.
- "まあ" has many meanings.
- It's used in various situations, like "まあいいか" when you want to say that something's not enough but you can put up with it, or "まあ試してみよう" when you think that something won't go well but you want to try it.
- It's also used in conversation without any particular meaning sometimes.

使い方 Usage

[1]「**まあ**、今日はこれくらいでやめておこうか。」
　　"Well, let's stop here for today."

[2]「テスト勉強全然してないから多分落ちるだろうけど、**まあ**受けてみるよ。」
　　"I haven't studied for the test at all so I'll probably fail, but, well, I'll give it a shot."

〜ないこともない

It's not that I don't 〜

例文 Example sentence  [No.52]

「あの店員さん、態度悪いね。私、文句言ってくる！」
「気持ちは**わからないこともない**けど、ちょっと落ち着いて。」

"That store clerk has a bad attitude. I'm gonna go make a complaint!"
"It's not that I don't get how you feel, but calm down a bit."

意味 Meaning

- 「ない」ということが「ない」、つまり、「〜だ」という意味
- 「食べないこともない」だったら、「食べない」ということを「しない」と言っているので、「食べる」という意味になる
- わざとこういう言い方をすることで、はっきり伝えたくない気持ちや自信がないという気持ちを表すことができる

- It's "not" that you "don't" do something, so it means that you "do" do it.
- If you say "食べたこともない" you're saying that you "don't" "not eat it," so it means you do eat it.
- By saying it like this on purpose, you can express feelings that you don't want to convey clearly or that you aren't confident in something.

使い方 Usage

[1]「ゆかの家の近くでご飯食べてるんだけど、今から来ない？」
「どうしようかなー。**行けないこともない**んだけど…明日朝早いからやめとく。」

"I'm having some food near your house, wanna come?"
"I'm not sure... It's not that I can't go, but ... I have to wake up early tomorrow, so I'll pass."

[2]「お酒は**飲めないこともない**んだけど、あんまり好きじゃないんだよね。」

"It's not that I can't drink alcohol, I just don't really like it."

にごす言葉 | Vague Words

〜とか

And 〜

例文 Example sentence [No.53]

「このあとみんなでカラオケとか、どう?」

「行こう!」

"How about we all go to karaoke or something after this?"
"Let's go!"

意味 Meaning

- 「〜とか〜とか」と例をあげるときに使う言葉
- 会話の中で「〜とか」のように1つだけで使うときは、確実ではないことやはっきり言いたくないことを言うときに使うことが多い
- あまり意味なく使うことがある言葉

- It's a word used when giving examples as in "〜とか〜とか"
- When you only use "〜とか" only once in a conversation, it's often used to say something that's not certain or that you don't want to say clearly.
- This is another word that's often used without much meaning.

使い方 Usage

[1]「この服とか、どう?似合うと思うんだけど。」

"How's this outfit and stuff? I think it goes well."

[2]「今日デートなのに、雨とか最悪…。」

"I have a date today, but this rain and stuff is the worst …"

〜けど
〜 but

例文 Example sentence [No.54]

「あの人見て！すごくかっこいいんだ**けど**！」
「ほんとだ！イケメン！」

"Check out that guy! He looks so cool!"
"You're right! He's so handsome!"

意味 Meaning

- 「だけど」や「けれども」を短く言った言葉で、「しかし」の意味を表す言葉
- 「けど…」と会話の最後につけると、少し気持ちを強調することがでる
- 「けど…」と会話を途中で終わらせて、後ろに続く言いたいことをはっきり言わないという使い方もある

- "けど" is a shortened form of "だけど" and "けれども, meaning "but."
- By adding "けど…" to the end of what you're saying, you can emphasize your feelings a bit.
- You can also use "けど…" to stop what you're saying in the middle, not clearly saying out loud what you want to say after.

使い方 Usage

[1]「なにこれ！めっちゃおいしいんだ**けど**！」

"What is this! But like, it's super delicious!"

[2]「それ、少し食べてみたいんだ**けど**…（少しくれない？）」

"I want to try a bite of that, but… (Can I have a little?)"

にごす言葉 | Vague Words

〜かな

I wonder 〜

例文 Example sentence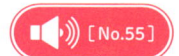

「どっちがいいかな?」

「私だったらこっちにするかな。」

"I wonder which one's better?"
"I think if it were me, I'd pick this one."

意味 Meaning

- 「これ、おいしいかな?」というように、「〜かどうかわからない」という意味で使われる言葉
- 会話では、文の終わりに「かな」をつけることで、少しやわらかく相手に意見を伝えることができる
- 「〜した方がいい」とアドバイスや注意をするときは、「〜した方がいいかな」と言うと、あまり強い印象を与えずやさしく伝えることができる

- This is a word used to mean "I don't know if something is … or not," as in "これ、おいしいかな?"
- In conversation, you can convey an opinion to the other person a bit more softly by adding "かな" at the end of the sentence.
- When giving advice or a warning that someone "〜した方がいい" something, you can say "〜した方がいいかな" so that you can convey it gently without giving off too strong of an impression.

使い方 Usage

[1]「ねぇ、どっちが似合う?」
　　「うーん、赤色がいいかな。」

"Hey, which one looks better on me?"
"Hmm, I think red might be better."

[2]「会議中はもう少し大きな声で話した方が、印象がよくなるかな、と思うよ。」

"I think speaking a bit louder during meetings might give a better impression."

「にごす言葉」について

　日本人は、はっきり意見を言ったり、誘いを断ったりすることが少ないと言われています。紹介したように、日本語には「にごす言葉」がたくさんありますよね。うまく使えば、相手を嫌な気持ちにさせない言い方をすることができますよ。でも、使いすぎると「はっきりしない」「自分の意見がない人」と思われてしまうこともあります。特に会社の会議のように意見をはっきり言う場では、使いすぎないように注意しましょう。

About "Vague Words"

　It's said that Japanese people rarely express clear opinions or decline invitations. As introduced before, there are many "vague words" in Japanese. Used properly, you can say things in a way that avoids making the other person feel unpleasant. However, if used too much, people may think that you're an "unclear" person or "someone who doesn't have their own opinion." Be careful not to overuse them, especially in situations where opinions are given distinctly, such as at work meetings.

クッション言葉

― Cushion Words ―

※クッション言葉：相手に自分の意見をやさしく伝えるための、
　クッションのような言葉
※Cushion words : Cushion-like words used to gently convey your opinion to the other person

もしよかったら…
If it's alright…

例文 Example sentence 〔No.56〕

「会社の隣に、新しくおしゃれなカフェができたらしいですよ。」
「そうなんですか！**もしよかったら**、一緒に行きませんか？」

"It seems that a fancy new cafe opened up next to the office."
"Is that so! If you'd like, we could go together?"

意味 Meaning

- 「もしあなたがOKだったら」という意味
- 何かお願いをするときや、相手を食事に誘うときなどにこの言葉をつけるとやわらかい印象になる
- 「もし（あなたが）よかったら」という言い方をした方が、相手が断りやすくなる
- 相手が断りやすい言い方をした方が、相手がプレッシャーを感じないので、印象がよくなることが多い

- This means "if it's okay with you."
- When asking for something or asking the other person out to eat, adding this phrase gives a soft impression.
- It's easier for the other party to decline if you say "もし（あなたが）よかったら"
- You won't pressure the other person if you say it in a way that makes it easy for them to refuse, and it gives a more positive impression of you.

使い方 Usage

[1] 「ゆか先生ですよね！**もしよかったら**、一緒に写真を撮ってもらえませんか？」
"You're Yuka-sensei, right? If it's alright, could I take a picture with you?"

[2] 「**もしよかったら**、明日一緒にお食事しませんか？」
"If you'd like, why don't we grab some food together tomorrow?"

クッション言葉 | Cushion Words

ポイント Point

「もしよかったら」の後ろには、「〜しましょう」「〜してください」などの文章が続きます。できるだけ「?」で終わる文章を続けた方が、よりやわらかい印象になりますよ。

After "もしよかったら" sentences follow with phrases like "〜しましょう" and "〜してください" Following it with sentences that end in questions wherever possible will give a softer impression.

似ているフレーズ Similar Phrases

● **もしよければ…** If it's alright...

「たら」が「ば」になりました。意味は全く同じです。

" たら " is changed to the " ば " form. The meaning is exactly the same.

● **もしよかったらでいいんですけど…** Only if it's alright with you...

「でいいんですけど…」と一緒に言うと、もっとやわらかい印象になります。

Combining the phrase with " でいいんですけど…" gives it a softer impression.

もしよければ、一緒にコーヒー買いに行かない?
If you don't mind, would you like to go buy some coffee with me?

いいね!
Sounds good!

フレーズ編 ③-14

悪いんだけど…

Sorry (to ask), but...

例文 Example sentence

「何か手伝いましょうか？」
「あ、じゃあ**悪いんだけど**、この仕事お願いしてもいい？」

"Can I help you with anything?"
"Oh, sorry to ask then, but could you handle this job for me?"

意味 Meaning

- 相手にお願いをするとき、よく一緒に使う言葉
- この「悪い」は、相手に対して「申し訳ない」という意味
- 何かお願いをすることで相手が時間や労力を使うことになるので、先にあやまる言い方

- It's a phrase that's often used together with a request to the other person.
- This "悪い" means you feel regretful toward the other person.
- The other person will spend their time and effort on you when you ask something of them, so this phrasing apologizes in advance.

使い方 Usage

[1]「**悪いんだけど**、手伝ってくれない？」
　　"Sorry, but could you help me?"

[2]「**悪いんだけど**、迎えに来てくれる？」
　　"Sorry, but could you come pick me up?"

[3]「**悪いんだけど**、先に帰ってもいい？ 頭が痛いんだ。」
　　"Sorry, but can I go home early? I have a headache."

クッション言葉 | Cushion Words

ポイント Point

特に相手にすごく迷惑をかけるときや、失礼なお願いをするときによく使います。「悪いんだけど…」をつけてお願いするときは、「申し訳ないと思っているけど、これをやってほしい！」と強く思っているので、相手は断わるのが難しくなります。「大変だと思うけど、あなたじゃないとできない」と思っているときに、この言葉を使いましょう。

It's often used especially when causing a great deal of trouble to the other person or when making an impolite request. When adding "悪いんだけど…" to your request, it means you strongly feel that "I'm sorry, but I want you to do this!" so it makes it difficult for the other person to decline. Use this phrase when you're thinking, "I know it's tough, but it has to be you."

似ているフレーズ Similar Phrases

● **申し訳ないんだけど…** I'm sorry, but...

意味は同じですが、「悪い」よりも少し丁寧な言い方です。

The meaning is the same, but it's a bit more polite than "悪い."

● **大変申し訳ありませんが… / 大変恐縮ですが…**

I'm very sorry, but... / I'm very sorry to bother you, but..

意味は同じですが、会社でよく使う言い方です。とても丁寧な言い方なので、友だちには使いません。

The meaning is the same, but these phrases are often used at work. It's a very polite way of saying it, so it's not used with friends.

せっかくなんだけど
I appreciate it, but...

例文 Example sentence [No.58]

「週末、会社のみんなでバーベキューするつもりなんだけど、村上さんもどう?」
「**せっかくなんだけど**、週末は予定があるんだ。誘ってくれてありがとう。」

"Everyone from the office is planning on having a barbecue this weekend. Would you like to come too, Murakami-san?"
"I appreciate it, but I have plans this weekend. Thanks for inviting me."

意味 Meaning

- 「誘ってもらえてとてもうれしいんだけど…」と言いながら、誘いを断るときに使う言葉
- 相手が自分のことを考えて誘ってくれたり、何かしてくれたことに対して、「ありがとう」の気持ちを伝えながら断ることができる

- It's a phrase used to refuse an invitation while saying, "I'm so happy you invited me, but…"
- It allows you to decline while conveying your feelings of thanks for an invitation or something the other person has done with you in mind.

使い方 Usage

[1]「このケーキ、ちょっと食べる?」
　　「**せっかくなんだけど**、今はいらないや。ダイエット中なんだ。」

"Want a bite of this cake?"
"Appreciate it, but not right now. I'm on a diet."

[2]「明日のイベント、参加できるよね?」
　　「**せっかくなんですが**、参加できないです…。すみません。」

"You can participate in tomorrow's event, right?"
"I appreciate it, but I won't be able to join… Sorry."

クッション言葉 | Cushion Words

ポイント Point

「せっかく」という言葉は「努力する」という意味があります。「いろんなことを乗り越えて何かを行う」という意味なので、「とてもうれしいけど、やめておきます」と誘いを丁寧に断るときに使う言葉です。

The word "せっかく" means "to make an effort." It means "doing something after having overcome various things," so it's used when politely refusing an invitation, as in "I'm so happy to be invited, but I'll pass."

似ているフレーズ Similar Phrases

● **せっかくだから…** Because it's a special XX...

「せっかくだからいただきます」「せっかくだから行きましょう」のように、「だから」と一緒に言うときは断るときには使いません。

When you say it together with "だから (because)" as in "せっかくだからいただきます (Because it's a special occasion, I'll have some)" or "せっかくだから行きましょう (Let's go, since it's a special chance,)" you can't use it when refusing something.

● **せっかくの○○なんだけど…** It's a special XX, but...

「せっかくのお誘いなんだけど」「せっかくの機会なんだけど」のように、具体的な言葉を入れて使うこともよくあります。

It's often used with concrete word or phrase, like "せっかくのお誘いなんだけど (It's a special invitation, but…)" or "せっかくの機会なんだけど (It's a special opportunity, but…)"

アイス買ってきたんだけど、食べる？
I bought ice cream, do you want some?

ありがとうございます！
せっかくだからいただきます。
Thank you! Because it's a special occasion, I'll have some.

個人的には…

Personally...

例文 Example sentence [No.59]

「この部屋の壁、緑色なんだ。かわいいね。」
「ありがとう。**個人的には**青色が好きなんだけどね。」

"Oh, the walls of your room are green. How cute."
"Thanks. Personally I like blue, though."

意味 Meaning

- 自分の意見や考えを伝えるときに使う
- 「まわりの意見ではなく、私だけの意見です」ということを強調する言い方
- 「絶対にこの意見が正しい」と思って言っているというよりも、「私はこう思いますが、他の人はわかりません」というように、少し弱く自分の意見を言うときに使うことが多い

- It's used to convey your own thoughts and opinions.
- It's a phrase that emphasizes that "it's my own opinion, not that of others."
- Rather than saying you think "this opinion is absolutely correct," it's often used to express your opinions a bit weakly, as in "I think this way, but I don't know about other people."

使い方 Usage

[1]「かみの毛切ったんだけど、みんなに似合わないって言われるんだ〜。」
　　「そう？**個人的には**前のかみ型より好きだけどな。」

"I cut my hair, but everyone's telling me it doesn't suit me."
"Really? Personally, I like it better than your last hairstyle."

[2]「このデザイン、どう思いますか？」
　　「かなりいいと思うよ。でも、**個人的には**全体的にもっと明るい色を使った方がよくなると思う。」

"What do you think of this design?"
"I think it's pretty good. But personally, I think it would be better to use brighter colors overall."

クッション言葉 | Cushion Words

ポイント Point

「自分の意見を言っているんだから、わざわざ『個人的』という言葉を使わなくてもいいんじゃない？」と思ったかもしれませんね。この言葉を使うときは「一般的な意見とはちょっと違うと思う」という気持ちで使うことが多いです。他にも、会議中に意見を言うときだったら、「この意見が正しいという証拠やデータはなくて、ただの私の感想ですが…」という意味で使います。

You might have thought, "I'm giving my own opinion, so do I have to bother using the word 'personally?'" This word is often used when feeling that "I think my opinion is a bit different from the general opinion." In addition, when giving an opinion during a meeting it's used to mean "I don't have any evidence or data that this opinion is correct, it's just a thought, but…"

似ているフレーズ Similar Phrases

● 直感では… My gut says...

「私が今感じたこと」という意味です。「そう思う理由ははっきり言えないけど、こう思う」と言いたいときに使います。

It means "what I've felt just now." It's used when you want to say, "I can't say exactly why I think this way, but I do."

● 感想としては… As for my impression...

情報やデータを参考にしたことではなく、「ただ私が思ったこと」を言うときに使われます。

It's used to say something is "just something I've thought," not that you've referred to any data or information.

知ってるかもしれないけど…

As you might know...

例文 Example sentence  [No.60]

「もう知ってるかもしれないけど、今日の会議、明日に変更になったよ。」
「さっき部長に聞いた。ありがとう。」

"You might already know, but today's meeting has been changed to tomorrow."
"I just heard from the department head. Thanks."

意味 Meaning

- 相手がすでに知っているかもしれないことを話すときに使う
- 「聞く」という動詞を使って、「聞いたかもしれないけど」と言っても同じ意味になる

- It's used when talking about things the other person might already know.
- "As you might have heard," using the verb "聞く (hear)" also has the same meaning.

使い方 Usage

[1]「知ってるかもしれないけど、あのお店来月閉店するんだって。」

"You might know, but I guess that store will close next month."

[2]「もう知ってるかもしれないけど、転職しようと思ってるんだよね。」

"You might already know, but I'm thinking about changing jobs."

[3]「もう聞いたかもしれないけど、実は先週からゆかちゃんと付き合ってるんだ。」

"As you might've heard, I've been going out with Yuka-chan since last week."

クッション言葉｜Cushion Words

ポイント Point

すでに知っていることを人に言われると「知っているよ！」と少し嫌な気持ちになるかもしれません。特に上下関係がある場合なら、失礼になることもあります。相手を嫌な気持ちにさせないために、この言葉を使います。だから、相手が知らないだろうな…と思うことだったとしても、「知ってるかもしれないけど」と言うことはよくあります。

You might feel a bit unpleasant when someone tells you something you already know, like "I know!" It can also come across as rude, especially in a hierarchical relationship. This word is used to avoid making the other person feel bad. That's why even if you think the other person doesn't know, it's common to say "知ってるかもしれないけど"

似ているフレーズ Similar Phrases

● 知ってると思うけど… I'm sorry, but...

「かもしれない」よりも、もっと知っている可能性が高いと思っているときに使います。

Used when you think there's a higher chance they know than with "かもしれない."

● ご存知だと思いますが… I'm sorry, but...

先生や上司にも使える丁寧な言い方です。

It's a polite way of saying it that can be used with teachers and bosses.

知ってると思うけど、そのお菓子、賞味期限切れてるよ。

I think you know, but those sweets have expired.

うん。気づいてたよ…

Yeah. I noticed. .

信じられないかもしれないけど…

Believe it or not...

例文 Example sentence [No.61]

「どうしたの？うれしそうだね。」

「うん！信じられないかもしれないけど、さっきカフェで『日本語の森』のゆか先生に会ったんだ！」

"What's going on? You look happy."
"Yeah! Believe it or not, I just met Yuka-sensei from 'Nihongo no Mori' at the cafe!"

意味 Meaning

- 相手がびっくりすることを言うときに使う
- 「信じられないくらい驚くと思うけど、本当の話なんだよ」と伝えたい気持ちや、「今からびっくりする話をするよ」と相手に伝えるために使う

- You use it when saying something that will surprise the other person.
- It's used to convey to the other person that you want to tell them something "so unbelievable that I think you're going to be surprised, but it's true," or that "I'm going to tell you something shocking right now."

使い方 Usage

[1]「信じられないかもしれないけど、N1に合格したんだ！」
　　"Believe it or not, I passed N1!"

[2]「信じられないかもしれないけど、宝くじに当たったんだ。」
　　"Believe it or not, I won the lottery."

[3]「信じられないかもしれないけど、昨日ゆかちゃんに告られた！」
　　"Believe it or not, Yuka-chan confessed her feelings for me yesterday!"

クッション言葉｜Cushion Words

ポイント Point

「信じられないかもしれないけど」と言っていますが、本当に相手に信じてもらえないと思っているわけではないことが多いです。「信じられないくらいびっくりする話を今からするよ！」という気持ちを表すときによく使います。本当に信じられないほど驚く話をすることは、あまりありませんからね。

You're saying "信じられないかもしれないけど" but most of the time it doesn't mean you really think that the other person won't believe you. It's often used to express the feeling that "I'm going to tell you something unbelievably surprising right now!" That's because there aren't many stories so surprising that you really can't believe them, right?

似ているフレーズ Similar Phrases

● **信じられないと思うけど…** I don't think you'll believe it, but…

「かもしれない」よりも、もっと信じてもらえない可能性が高いと思っているときに使います。

You use this when you think there's a higher chance they won't believe you than with "かもしれない."

● **びっくりすると思うけど…** I think you'll be surprised, but…

「信じられない」より、会話でよく使います。

Used more often in conversation than "信じられない."

● **あり得ないと思うかもしれないけど…** You might think it's impossible, but…

「そんなことが起きるなんて絶対にないと思うだろうけど…」という意味です。

It means "You probably think something like this would never happen, but…"

〜したんだけど…

I did 〜, and...

例文 Example sentence [No.62]

「先週の日本語の試験、**受けてみたんだけど**全然できなかったよ。」
「まだ結果出てないんでしょ？合格かもしれないよ。」

"I tried taking the Japanese test last week, but I couldn't answer the questions at all."
"You haven't got the results yet, right? You might've passed."

意味 Meaning

- 自分が経験したことを説明するときに、よく使う
- この「だけど」に反対の意味はない。「〜して、それで…」のように文をつなぐことができる

- You often use this to describe what you've experienced.
- The "だけど" here doesn't indicate contrast.
  It allows you to connect sentences together like with "〜して、それで…(〜, and then...)"

使い方 Usage

[1]「昨日遊園地に**行ったんだけど**、すごく楽しかった！」
　　"I went to the amusement park yesterday and it was a lot of fun!"

[2]「自分でお弁当を**作ったんだけど**、すごくおいしくできた！」
　　"I made my own bento box and it was really delicious!"

[3]「さっき公園に**行ったんだけど**、小学生でいっぱいだったよ。」
　　"I went to the park earlier and it was full of elementary school students."

クッション言葉 | Cushion Words

ポイント Point

話し始めるときに「〜したんだけど…」と言うと、「今からこのことについて話します」と聞く人に知らせることができます。これを言うと、相手は話を聞きやすくなりますよ。

If you say "〜したんだけど…" when you start talking, you can alert the listener that "I'm going to talk about this topic now." Saying this makes it easier for the other person to listen to your story.

似ているフレーズ Similar Phrases

● **〜さ** Right? (as a filler word)

「昨日遊園地に行ってさ、すごく楽しかった！」のように、「さ」も文をつなぐことができます。
"さ" can also connect sentences, as in "昨日遊園地に行ってさ、すごく楽しかった！(I went to the amusement park yesterday, right? And it was lots of fun!)"

> 先週とった動画アップロードしたんだけど、
> 再生回数いい感じだよ！
>
> I uploaded the video we took last week,
> and it's getting a good number of views!

> うれしいですねー！
>
> I'm so glad!

「クッション言葉」について

　日本人の会話では、はっきり自分の考えを言わない場面が多いです。あまりはっきり意見を言ってしまうと、言われた人が傷ついたり嫌な気持ちになることがあるからです。外国の人から見ると「はっきり言わないから何が言いたいのかわからない」と思うかもしれませんが、日本人にとっては「クッション言葉」や「にごす言葉」を使うことが、相手への優しさでもあるんです。どんなに正しいことを言っていたとしても、言い方が悪ければ意見を聞いてもらえないということもありますよね。また、相手のお願いの仕方が悪ければ、そのお願いを引き受けたくないと思うことは、みなさんにもあると思います。日本語の会話では、こういう言葉をうまく使うことで、自分の意見を聞いてもらいやすくなります。お願いを引き受けてもらいやすくなりますよ。相手のため、そして自分のためにも、この「クッション言葉」を使えるようになると便利だと思います。

　特にビジネスの世界では、紹介した言葉以外にも「クッション言葉」がたくさん使われています。「相手への優しさ」というより、「決まった言い方」として使われることが多いですね。だから言わないと失礼になることもあります。日本人は大人になって働き始めてから、先輩の話し方を聞いて「クッション言葉」を勉強していきます。だから、みなさんが難しいと感じるのは当然だと思いますよ。

About "Cushion Words"

In Japanese conversations, there are many situations where people don't express their own thoughts clearly. That's because giving your opinion too distinctly may hurt the other person or make them feel unpleasant. From a foreigner's point of view, you may think, "I don't know what Japanese people mean because they don't say things clearly," but for them, using "cushion words" and "vague words" is a form of kindness toward the other person. No matter how correct something you've said is, people sometimes won't listen to you if your phrase things poorly, right? Also, I don't think anyone would want to take on something asked of you if the request was made poorly. Using these words well in Japanese conversation will make it easier for your opinion to be heard. It'll also make it easier to get people to agree to your requests. I think that learning how to use these "cushion word" is handy for the sake of the both other person and yourself as well.

Many "cushion words" are used aside from the phrases introduced here, especially in the business world. They're often used as a fixed way of saying something rather than as a form of kindness to the other person. So not saying them can come off as rude. After becoming an adult and starting work, Japanese people learn "cushion words" by listening how their seniors speak. So I think it's natural for you all to find them difficult.

怒るときの言葉
おこ　　　　　　　ことば

― Words for when Angry ―

怒るときの言葉 | Words for when Angry

なんで？
How come?

例文 Example sentence [No.63]

「今日の服、あまり似合ってないね。かみの毛も切ったんだ。前の方がよかったな。」
「**なんで**そんなことばっかり言うの？」

"Your outfit doesn't look so good today. Oh, you cut your hair too. It looked better before."
"Why do you always say things like that?"

意味 Meaning

- 「どうして？」と理由を聞くときに使う言葉
- 怒っているときに使う「なんで？」は、理由を聞いていると言うよりも「怒っています」という気持ちを表すときに使う

- This word is used when asking a reason why.
- Saying "なんで？" when angry expresses that you're feeling upset more so than asking for a reason.

使い方 Usage

［1］「**なんで**こんなこともわからないの？」

　　"How come you can't even understand this?"

［2］「ごめん。借りてた本なくしちゃった。」
　　「**なんで**？意味わからない。ちゃんと返してよ。」

　　"Sorry. I lost the book I borrowed from you."
　　"How come? I don't get what you mean. Just get it back to me."

むかつく
Annoyed / Annoying

例文 Example sentence  [No.64]

「さっきレジに並んでたら、いきなりおばさんが私の前に入ってきたんだ。」
「えー！そういうの、**むかつく**よね。」

"As I was just lining up at the register, some old lady suddenly cut in front of me."
"What! That stuff's so annoying."

意味 Meaning

- 嫌な気持ち、特に怒ったときに使う言葉
- 「怒っています」という気持ちをはっきり伝えることができる
- You use this word for unpleasant feelings, especially when you've gotten upset.
- It allows you to clearly convey that you're feeling angry.

使い方 Usage

[1]「昨日部長が私の悪口を大声で言ってたんだよね。」
　　「なにそれ。**むかつく**ね。」

"My department head was insulting me out loud yesterday."
"What the heck? So irritating."

[2]「ちょっとこのごみ、捨てておいてくれる？」
　　「は？なんであなたに命令されなきゃいけないの？**むかつく**。」

"Hey, could you help throw this garbage away?"
"Huh? How come I have to be bossed around by you? So annoying."

怒るときの言葉 | Words for when Angry

ふざけないで
Don't mess around.

例文 Example sentence　[No.65]

「そんなに怒らないでよ〜。笑って笑って！」
「**ふざけないで**よ。真剣に話してるんだから。」

"Don't get so angry. Smile! Smile!"
"Don't mess around. I'm being serious."

意味 Meaning

- 「ふざける」は、冗談を言ったり、遊んだりして真面目ではない状態を表す言葉
- 本当に相手がふざけていた場合だけではなく、ふざけてはいなくても、相手にもっと真剣に考えてほしいと思うときにも使う
- 「ふざけんなよ」や「ふざけてるの？」という言い方もある

- "ふざける" is a word that describes a joking, playful, and non-serious situation.
- It's used not only when the other person really is messing around, but also even when they're not and you want them to take something more seriously.
- It can also be phrased as "ふざけんなよ (Don't mess around)" or "ふざけてるの?(Are you messing with me?)"

使い方 Usage

[1]「資料確認したけど、ミスが多すぎる。**ふざけてる**？全部やり直して。」
　　「はい。申し訳ありませんでした。」

"I checked the materials and there are too many mistakes. Are you messing around? Redo everything."
"Understood. My apologies."

[2]「ゆかは頭が悪いから、まあ合格なんてできないと思うけど。」
　　「なに？**ふざけてるの**？」

"You're dumb, so, well, I don't think you can pass."
"What? Are you joking?"

ありえない！
No way!

例文 Example sentence [No.66]

「ごめん！今起きた。1時間くらい遅れると思う…。」
「は？ありえない！もう今日はデートしない！」

"Sorry! I just got up. I think I'll be about an hour late…"
"What? No way! I'm not going on a date with you today anymore!"

意味 Meaning

- 「〜えない」は「〜できない」と言う意味なので、「そんなことが起こるはずがない！」という強い気持ちを表す言葉
- 相手の言ったことやしたことが悪い、よくないと言いたいときに使う
- 同じ意味で「信じられない！」もよく使う

- "〜えない" means "not possible," so this word expresses strong feelings that "something like that can't happen!"
- You use it when you want to say that what the other person has said or done is that bad.
- "信じられない！(I can't believe it!)" is also often used in the same way.

使い方 Usage

[1]「そろそろお兄ちゃんのこと、許してあげたら？」
  「ありえないでしょ。一生許さない。」

  "Isn't it about time you forgive your brother?"
  "There's no way. I won't forgive him for the rest of my life."

[2]「あれ？なんか今日いつもよりかわいくないな。」
  「信じられない！なんでそんなこと言うの？！」

  "Huh? You're like, not as cute as usual today."
  "I can't believe you! Why would you say that?!"

怒るときの言葉 | Words for when Angry

いらいらする

Frustrating

例文 Example sentence [No.67]

「ゆか、まだ来ないね。寝てるんじゃない？」
「そうだよね。電話しても出ないし。もういらいらする！」

"Yuka hasn't come yet. I bet she's sleeping."
"You're right. She's not even answering the phone. So irritating!"

意味 Meaning

- 自分のやりたいことがうまくできなかったり、相手に何かをされたりして嫌な気持ちになったときに使う言葉
- 「むかつく」と同じように、「今怒っています」とはっきり表すことができる言葉

- This word is used when you can't properly do something that you want to, or when someone does something that makes you feel uncomfortable.
- It allows you to clearly express that you're angry, just like with "むかつく."

使い方 Usage

[1]「うわ〜道がすごく混んでいる。いらいらするなあ。」

"Wow, this road is jam packed. So irritating."

[2]「もうお腹すいた！早くご飯食べたい！早く！」
「わかった、わかった。そんなにいらいらしないで。」

"I'm hungry already! I want to eat something quick! Quick!"
"Alright, alright. Don't get so irritated."

バカにしてる？
Are making fun of me?

例文 Example sentence [No.68]

「これ、できる？」
「**バカにしてる**？ できるに決まってるじゃん。」

"Can you do this?"
"Are you making a fool of me? Of course I can."

意味 Meaning

- 「バカにする」は「相手を下に見る」という意味がある
- 相手に「下に見られている」とか「軽く見られている」と感じる行動や発言をされたときに使う
- 「バカにしてる？」や「バカにしないで！」という言い方もある

- "バカにする" means "looking down on the other person."
- It's used when the other person does or says something that makes you feel "looked down on" or "viewed lightly."
- You can also phrase it as "バカにしてる？(Are you making fun of me?)" or "バカにしないで！(Don't make fun of me!)"

使い方 Usage

[1]「この本面白いよ。あ、でもゆかにはちょっと難しいかも。」
「**バカにしないで**。」

"This book is interesting. Oh, but it might be a bit difficult for you, Yuka."
"Don't make fun of me."

[2]「すごい！ひらがなが読めるんだね！」
「**バカにしてる**？こんなの簡単だよ。」

"Wow! You can read hiragana!"
"Are you making fun of me? It's easy."

怒るときの言葉 | Words for when Angry

もういい！
Enough!

例文 Example sentence [No.69]

「ごめん。許して。」
「**もういい**。顔も見たくない。」

"I'm sorry. Forgive me."
"Enough. I don't even want to see your face."

意味 Meaning

- 「もう必要ないです」「もうあきらめます」という意味
- 何かお願いをしたのに、それを聞いてくれないときや、話を聞いてくれないときによく使う

- It means you "I don't need something anymore" or "I give up already."
- It's often used when the other person won't do something you've asked of them, or when they're won't listen to what you're saying.

使い方 Usage

[1]「先生、授業に遅れてすみません。
あと、宿題を忘れちゃって…教科書も家に忘れました…。」
「そうですか。**もういい**です。教室から出て行ってください。」

"Sensei, sorry I'm late to class. Also, I forgot my homework… I forgot my textbook at home, too…"
"Is that so? Enough. Please get out of my classroom."

[2]「ねえ、なんでそんなに怒ってるの？」
「**もういい**。ほっといて。」

"Hey, why are you so angry?"
"Enough. Just leave me alone."

日本人が怒るとき

いつもは敬語を使わない相手に対して、敬語を使って怒る場面を見たことはありませんか？ アニメや漫画でも、よくあると思います。敬語を使う相手は、先生や上司や初対面の人ですよね。つまり、敬語はあまり親しくない人に対して使います。だから、けんかをしたときに「もうやめてもらえますか？」のようにわざと丁寧な言い方をすると「あなたとは今仲良くありません」という気持ちを表すことができます。私の母は、父とけんかしたときに、よく丁寧な言い方を使っていました！丁寧な言い方で怒られる方が、もっとこわいんですよね…。

When Japanese people get angry

Have you ever seen someone who doesn't usually use honorific language use it when they're angry? I think it's a common sight even in anime and manga. You use honorifics with people like teachers, bosses, and people you've met for the first time. That is to say, honorifics are used toward people you're not very close with. When you're in a fight, you can express feeling that "we're not on good terms right now" by deliberately speaking politely, as in "Could you kindly stop?" My mother used to speak politely whenever she bickered with my father! It's even scarier when someone gets mad at you in a polite tone…

気持ちを表す言葉
― Words to Express Feelings ―

疲れたー！
I'm tired!

「疲れたー！」には、たくさんの言い方があります。
"疲れたー！" has various way to say.

例文 Example sentence 　[No.70]

「ただいまー！あぁ、**もう動けないよ**。」
「お疲れ様。」

"I'm home! Ah, I can't even move anymore."
"Good job today."

いろいろな言い方 Various ways of phrasing it

だるー　Blah/sluggish

- 「だるい」は「体を動かしたくない」というときに使う言葉
- 「なんとなく疲れた」「やらなければいけないことがあるけど、やるのがめんどくさい」と思っているときにもよく使う

- "だるい" is a word used when you don't want to move your body.
- It's also often used when you feel tired for some reason or have something to do, but can't be bothered.

しんどい　Blah/sluggish

- 何もしたくないくらい疲れているときに使う
- 心よりも、体が疲れているときに使うことが多い

- This is used when you're so tired that you don't want to do anything.
- It's used more often when you're physically tired rather than mentally.

気持ちを表す言葉 | Words to Express Feelings

しんど Blah/sluggish

- 「しんどい」を短く言った言葉
- It's a shortened form of the word for "しんどい."

もう動けない I can't even move anymore.

- 「もう動けない」と思うくらい疲れているときに使う言葉
- 「本当に動けないということはないんだけど、少しも動けないと思うくらい疲れている」という意味になる
- This word is used when you're so tired that you think, "I can't even move anymore."
- It doesn't really mean that you can't move, but it means that you're so tired that you feel like you can't even move a little bit.

もう無理 "I can't anymore."

- 「無理」は「できない」という意味。もう動けない、走れない、働けない…など、これ以上できないことを伝えるときに使う
- "無理" means "impossible." It's used to convey that you can't do something anymore, as in you can't move anymore, run anymore, work anymore, etc.

使い方 Usage

[1] 学校行くのだるー。
Going to school is so tiresome.

[2] はぁー！しんどい。
Ahh! So tiresome.

[3] もう無理。何もしたくないよー。
I can't anymore. I don't want to do anything.

163

つらい
Tough / gruesome

「つらい」には、たくさんの言い方があります。
"つらい" has various way to say.

例文 Example sentence [No.71]

「彼から返事こないし、**もう無理**。私のこと好きじゃなくなったのかな…。」
「そんなことないと思うよ。」

"My boyfriend won't reply to me, I can't do this anymore. I wonder if he doesn't like me anymore..."
"I don't think that's the case."

いろいろな言い方 Various ways of phrasing it

つら Tough/gruesome
- 「つらい」を短く言った言葉
- A shortened form of the word "つらい (tough/gruesome.)"

つらすぎ Too tough/gruesome
- 「〜すぎる」は「とても〜だ」という意味。「とてもつらい」という意味になる
- "〜すぎる" means "very 〜." This means "very tough/gruesome."

もう、涙出てくる I'm gonna cry already
- まだ泣いていないんだけど、泣きそうなくらいつらいというときに使う
- 「もう泣きそう」という言い方もある
- You use this when you haven't cried yet, but when something's so tough/gruesome that you feel you're about to.
- You can also phrase it as "もう泣きそう (I'm about to cry)."

気持ちを表す言葉 | Words to Express Feelings

もう無理 I can't anymore.

- 「疲れた」の意味でも使うが、「もうこれ以上がんばれない…」という意味でも使う
- 「がんばれないほど心が弱っていてつらい」という意味
- It can also be used to mean "tired," but it can even be used to mean "I can't push on anymore…"
- It means it's so tough and my heart is so weakened that I can't push on.

もういや I'm done

- つらいことがあって、もう何もしたくないと言うときに使う
- You use this when saying that something tough/gruesome happened and you don't want to do anything anymore.

最悪 Terrible

- 「1番悪い」という意味。とても嫌なことやつらいこと、苦しいことがあったときに使う言葉
- Since it means "the worst," this word is used when there's been something very unpleasant, tough/gruesome, or distressing.

使い方 Usage

[1] あー、**つら**。泣きそうだよ。
　　Ahh, it's so tough. I'm about to cry.

[2] 宿題こんなにあるの…**もういや**。
　　I have so much homework to do… I'm done with this.

[3] **最悪**。スマホの画面われた。
　　This sucks. My phone screen cracked.

おいしい！
Delicious!

「おいしい！」には、たくさんの言い方があります。
"おいしい！" has various way to say.

例文 Example sentence [No.72]

「やば！なにこれ！」

「ね！おいしすぎる！」

"Crazy good! What is this!"
"Right! It's so delicious!"

いろいろな言い方 Various ways of phrasing it

おいしすぎる So delicious

- 「〜すぎる」は「とても〜だ」という意味
- 「めっちゃおいしい」よりも、もっとおいしいと思っているように聞こえる
- "〜すぎる" means "very 〜."
- It sounds like you think something's even more delicious than when you say "めっちゃおいしい (very delicious)."

うまい！/ うまっ！/ うんま！ So good!

- あまりきれいな言葉ではないが、友だちにはよく言う
- 食べ物を食べたとき、すぐに言うことが多い言葉
- It's not a very pretty word, but it's often used with friends.
- It's often said immediately after taking a bite of food.

気持ちを表す言葉 | Words to Express Feelings

やばっ！ Crazy good!

- どんな形容詞にも使うことができる「やばい」を短く言った言葉
- とてもおいしい！と感動した気持ちを表すときに使う
- 友だちだけに使う

- It's a shortened form of the word for "やばい," which can be used with any adjective.
- It's used to express feeling impressed that something is "so delicious!"
- You should also try to only use this with friends.

なにこれ！ What is this!

- 本当に「これは何？」と思っているわけではない
- 「今まで食べたことがないくらい、おいしいものだ！」という気持ちを込めて使う言葉

- It doesn't really mean you're wondering what something is.
- The phrase is used when you feel that something is "so delicious, you've never had anything like it before."

最高！ Awesome!

- 「1番おいしい」と思ったときに使う

- You use this when you think something is "the best."

使い方 Usage

[1] このケーキ、**おいしすぎる**！

This cake is so good!

[2] **うまっ！なにこれ**！

Crazy good! What is this!

[3] やっぱりお母さんのご飯、**最高**！

Mom's cooking is still the best!

みんなでお昼ごはんを食べに行こう

Let's all go out for lunch

 [No.73]

ゆか先生！
もう**知ってるかもしれないですけど**、
会社の近くに新しいラーメン屋さんできたんですよ。

Yuka-sensei!
You might already know, but a new ramen shop opened up near the office.

へえ〜。

Oh, really...

え？ゆか先生ラーメン好きですよね？
興味ないですか？

Huh? Yuka-sensei, you like ramen, don't you?
Aren't you interested?

うーん。なんか、今日朝から頭痛いんだよね。

Umm... I've had, like, a headache since this morning.

なるほど、だからそんなリアクションなんですね。

I see, so that's why you reacted like that.

まあ、食べ**られないこともない**けど…。
せっかくだけど、今日はやめとこうかな。

Well, it's not that I couldn't go eat ramen,
I appreciate the invite, but I think I'll pass today.

その方がいいですね。
店員さんめっちゃイケメンだった**けど**…。

It's probably better that way.
The staff were really handsome, though...

え？そうなの？
なんか、元気になってきた！行こっか！

Huh? Is that so?
I'm feeling better somehow! Let's go!

（なに、この人…。）

(What's up with this person...)

みんな、ラーメン好き？
私は毎日でも食べたいくらい大好き！
日本のラーメンには、みそ味・しょうゆ味・しお味など、
他にもいろんな味があるんだよ。

Do you all like ramen?
I love it so much that I want to have it every day!
There are so many different kinds of Japanese ramen,
like miso, soy sauce, salt-flavored, and more.

会話 ③-2 ゆか先生はラーメンが大好き!

Yuka-sensei loves ramen!

[No.74]

あー！もう、**いらいらする**！

Ah! I'm so irritated!

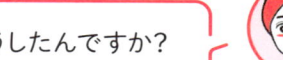

どうしたんですか？

What happened?

あのラーメン屋さん行ったんだけど、
1時間待ってやっと食べられると思ったら、
「スープがなくなったから今日はお店閉めます」だって。
むかつくー！食べたかったのに！

I went to that ramen shop, and when I thought I could finally eat after waiting for an hour, they said, "We ran out of soup, so we're closing the shop for today." So annoying! I wanted to have it!

えー！**ありえない**ですね！

What! No way!

っていうか、まだ12時だよ？
12時でスープなくなる**とか**…準備してなさすぎ！

I mean, it's still only 12 o'clock, you know?
Running out of soup and stuff at 12 o'clock…they're way too unprepared!

もしよかったら、別の店舗行きます？
車で1時間くらいのところにあるみたいですよ。

If you'd like, want to go to a different location? It seems there's one about an hour's drive away.

いいね！行こう！

Nice! Let's go!

あ、でも午後から会議が･･･。

Oh, but there's a meeting this afternoon...

あー**悪いんだけど**、会議は明日に変更って
みんなに言っといてくれる？早くラーメン行こう！

Oh, sorry, but could you tell everyone that the meeting's been changed to tomorrow? Let's go get some ramen quick!

大丈夫**かな**･･･。

I wonder if that's okay...

「ラーメンを食べるのに1時間も待つの?!」と
びっくりしたかもしれないけど、
有名なラーメン屋さんなら、よくあることですよ。
私は2時間待ったこともあります！

You might've been surprised, thinking,
"They'd wait an hour to eat ramen?!"
but it's common at famous ramen shops.
I've even waited 2 hours before!

ごちそうさま！でも…。

Thanks for the meal! But...

[No.75]

なにこれ！おいしすぎる！

What is this! It's so delicious!

ここのラーメン、おいしいですね！
まあ、個人的にはもう少しあっさりした味の方が好きですけど。

The ramen here is delicious, right?!
Well, personally I prefer a slightly lighter flavor, though.

確かに、**わからないこともない**な。
ちょっと**重い**よね。

For sure, I get what you mean. It's a bit rich.

っていうか、おいしいけど値段高いですよね。

By the way, it's delicious but it's pricey.

まあ、他の店に比べたらちょっと高い**かなーみたいな
感じ**はするよね。

Well, it feels like it might be a bit pricier compared to other places.

はい。でも**まあ**、味はやっぱり**最高**です！
Right. But, well, the flavor is still amazing!

よし！じゃあ帰ろっか。
あの…本当に**申し訳ない**んだけど…。
Alright! Shall we head home, then? Err... I'm really sorry, but...

財布忘れた、ですか？
Did you forget your wallet?

え、よくわかったね！**すごい！さすが！**
Huh, how'd you know! Brilliant, as expected!

なんでいつも忘れるんですか…。
もういいです。お金払っとくんで、早く帰りましょう。
How come you always forget it...
Enough already. I'll pay, so let's go home already.

日本のラーメンは、
1杯600円〜800円くらいのものが多いかな。
お店によっては、500円以下で食べられるものや
1500円くらいするラーメンもあるよ。
I think most Japanese ramen is about 600 to 800 yen per bowl.
Depending on the shop, you can also get ramen for
under 500 yen or ramen that costs around 1,500 yen.

あいづちの役割

　あいづちをうつのは「あなたの話をしっかり聞いていますよ」ということを、相手に伝えるためです。あいづちがあると、話している人は安心して話し続けることができます。逆にあいづちがないと、「話の内容が理解できていないのかな？」「私の話が面白くないのかな？」「もしかして、私のことが嫌い…？」と、色々なことを考えてしまって、不安になってしまいます。みなさんの国では、どのようにあいづちをうちますか？もしかしたら、日本人が会話の中であいづちをうつ回数は、他の国の人よりも多いかもしれませんね。あいづちやクッション言葉は、日本人にとっては相手への「気づかい」です。相手が不安にならないように、気持ちよく話せるように使うものです。ただ、あいづちもうてばいいというものではありません。適当なあいづちをうち続けると、相手は「私に興味がないんだ」と感じます。よいコミュニケーションをとるためには、まず相手に興味をもって、それをあいづちや表情で伝えることが大切です。これは日本語に限らず、どこの国でも同じなのではないでしょうか。

The role of aizuchi interjections

The purpose of using aizuchi (interjections) is to let the other person know that "I'm listening to your story." Using aizuchi lets the speaker keep going with peace of mind. On the flip side, without aizuchi, they'll worry and think a lot of things like "Do they not understand the content of my story?" "I wonder if what I'm saying isn't interesting?" or "Maybe they hate me...?" How do you use interjections in your country? It may be that Japanese people use interjections more times during conversation than people in other countries do. To Japanese people, aizuchi and cushion words are a form of "consideration" toward the other person. They're used so that the other person can speak comfortably and won't get anxious. But it doesn't mean that it's good enough to just use aizuchi. If you keep using them randomly, the other person will feel that you're not interested in them. To maintain good communication, it's important to first be interested in the other person and convey that interest through aizuchi or facial expressions. Isn't this the same in every country, not just for Japanese?

「あいづち」は「あいづちをうつ」と言うよ。
「あいづちをする」
「あいづちを言う」は
使えないから気をつけてね。

You "hit or strike (うつ)" aizuchi.
Be careful, because you can't "do (する)" or "say (言う)" aizuchi.

便利な形容詞「やばい」

「やばい」は、もともと「危ない」という意味です。悪いことが起こりそうなときに使う言葉でした。でも最近では、おいしいものを食べたときにも「やばい」、かっこいい人を見たときにも「やばい」、すごいものを見たときにも「やばい」と言います。だいたいの形容詞は「やばい」という言葉で表現できるのではないでしょうか。すごく便利な言葉ではありますが、「やばい」ばかりを使っていると、自分を表現するための語彙力がどんどん下がってしまいます… 使い過ぎには注意しましょうね。

The useful adjective "やばい"

The original meaning of "やばい" is "dangerous," and it was used when something bad was about to happen. But lately, you can say "やばい" when you eat delicious food, "やばい" when you see cool people, and "やばい" when you see something amazing. I bet that most adjectives can be expressed using the word "やばい." It's a really convenient word to use, but if you only ever say "やばい," your vocabulary for expressing yourself will steadily decrease... Be careful not to overuse it.

ゆか先生のおすすめ勉強法

Tips for studying Japanese

「日本語を勉強する」といっても、その目的によって勉強方法が変わります。目的をしっかり確認して、勉強方法を決めましょう！

Even if you say you're going to study Japanese, your study methods will differ depending on your goals. Get a firm grasp on your goals and decide on a study method!

日本語能力試験に合格したい人へ

For those who want to pass an exam

試験には、漢字・語彙・文法・読解・聴解の能力を試す問題が出てきますが、どれが1番大切だと思いますか？ 正解は、漢字です！

漢字が嫌いって言う人がすごく多いんですが、漢字は全ての能力のもとになるものです。漢字が組み合わさったものが語彙で、語彙とひらがなの組み合わせが文法ですよね。そして、語彙と文法の組み合わせで文章ができています。

Exams will have questions that test your kanji, vocabulary, grammar, reading comprehension, and listening comprehension, but which do you think is the most important? The correct answer is kanji!

Many people say they hate kanji, but they're the basis of all Japanese language abilities. Vocabulary is a combination of different kanji, and grammar is a combination of vocabulary and hiragana. And sentences are made up of a combination of vocabulary together with grammar.

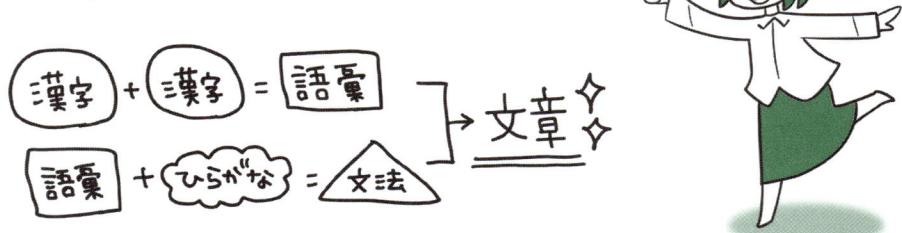

え？　漢字をどう覚えるかって？　おすすめは漢字をストーリーで覚えることです！
「日本語の森」ではストーリーを作って面白く漢字を覚える授業をしています。ぜひ、「日本語の森」の授業を受けてみてくださいね！

Huh? How should you learn kanji? Our recommendation is to learn them through stories! At 'Nihongo no Mori,' we have a class where we come up with stories to make learning kanji interesting. Please be sure to try out a class at 'Nihongo no Mori'!

A parent is standing on a tree looking at their children.

ひらがなやカタカナ、アルファベットなどは"音"を表す文字ですよね。
でも漢字は"意味"を表す文字です。
例えば「火」という漢字を知っていれば、「焼」「燃」「炒」などの漢字も「火に関係がある漢字なんだな」とわかりますね。初めて見た漢字で読み方がわからなくても、意味が想像できるのが漢字の面白いところですよ。

Hiragana, katakana, and the alphabet are characters that represent "sound", aren't they? But kanji are characters that represent "meaning".
For example, if you know the kanji "fire", you can understand that the kanji such as "焼", "燃", and "炒" are also "characters related to fire". The interesting thing about kanji is that you can imagine their meaning even if you don't know how to read them.

会話が上手になりたい人へ

For those who want to get better at conversation

私が今まで出会ってきた学習者の中で「日本語が本当に上手だな」と思った人に共通していることは、「まね」をしているということです。

Among all of the Japanese learners I've met, what those I think are truly good at it have in common is that they imitate.

● 例えば…

有名な方法ですが、「シャドーイング」はかなり効果が高いと思います。「シャドーイング」は、**流れる音声を追いかけるように声を出して読む勉強方法**のことです。実は私も英語を勉強したときは、「シャドーイング」をしていました。

"Shadowing" is a famous learning method, and I think it's quite effective. It's a study method where you read out loud as though your following the voice that's being played. Actually, when I studied English, I practiced "shadowing."

会話の練習をしている人は、単語1つ1つの発音を気にしている人が多いですが、会話では単語1つの発音よりも、**文章全体のイントネーションがすごく大切**だと思います。単語の意味がはっきりわからなくても、とにかく**会話のリズムを体に覚えさせる**と、自然な日本語が話せるようになりますよ！

Many people who practice conversation worry about the pronunciation of each and every word, but I think that in conversation, the intonation of the entire sentence is extremely important, more so than the pronunciation of each individual word. Even if you don't clearly understand the meaning of a word, if you force your body to learn the rhythm of conversations in any case, you'll become able to speak natural Japanese!

「会話編」を使って、ぜひシャドーイングをしてみてね！

Be sure to try shadowing using the "Conversation" series!

▶ おすすめのYouTube番組
Recommended YouTube Show

日本語の森ch

── 01 ──

【日本語が上達したあなたへ】
こんな日本語、使ってしまっていませんか？
相手への印象を良くする言い方5選！

#日本語 #Japanese

動画は
こちらから！

この本を作るきっかけにもなった動画です。
今まで学生と関わる中で「これ、みんなよく間違っているな」と思ったものをまとめて紹介しています。ここで紹介している表現は、言葉の意味や文法が間違っているわけではないので、なかなか気付きにくいし注意してくれる人も少ないと思います。少し上級者向けですが、日本人と関わることがある人なら、明日からでも使えるものが見つかると思います。

This video also inspired me to make this book.
In it, I introduce all the things that I've thought that everybody keeps getting wrong while working with students up until now. The meaning of the words and the grammar in the the expressions I introduce here aren't necessarily incorrect, so they're hard to notice and I think few people would ever tell you. It's aimed a bit more toward advanced learners, but if you're someone who interacts with Japanese people, I believe you'll find something that you can use even starting from tomorrow.

02

Lemon / 米津玄師
【日本の歌で日本語を勉強しよう #01】

#Lemon　#米津玄師　#Japanesesong

動画は
こちらから！

日本で人気の歌を紹介する動画です。

歌詞は、言葉の意味がわかったとしても、どういうことが言いたいのかわからないものが多いですよね。この動画では、言葉の意味だけではなく、歌詞の中でどんな意味で使われているのかも説明しています。【日本の歌で日本語を勉強しよう】はシリーズになっていて、他にもいろいろな曲を紹介していますよ。ちなみに、このシリーズには英語とトルコ語の字幕がついているものがあります。これは動画を見ている学生が作ってくれたものです。もしできるなら、自分の言語で字幕を作ってみてね。勉強にもなるよ！

This video introduces a song that's popular in Japan.
With lyrics, it's often hard to understand what they're trying to say even if you understand the meaning of each word. In this video, we explain not only the words' definitions, but also what they're used to mean in the lyrics.
"Let's study Japanese through songs" is a series, and we also have videos introducing many other different songs.
By the way, some of the videos in this series have English and Turkish subtitles. They were made by students who watch our videos. If you can, try making subtitles in your own language. It's good for studying, too!

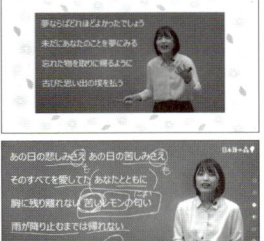

あとがき

みなさん、楽しんでいただけましたか?

この本は、私が日本語学習者と直接触れ合って感じたことや、YouTubeやSNS上のコメント、みんながいつも送ってくれるメッセージや質問を参考にして作りました。日本語教師になったばかりのころは、みんなが日本語のどういうところを難しいと思っているのかがまったくわかりませんでした。でも、YouTubeでライブをしたときに直接みんなの反応を見ることができたし、たくさんのコメントやメッセージ（いいものも悪いものも全部！）をもらったおかげで、少しはいい先生に近づけたのかな？と思っています。今回本を書く機会に恵まれたのも、みなさんが私を日本語の先生として育ててくれたからだと思っています。

このような素敵な機会を与えてくださったアスク出版のみなさま、「日本語の森」や「ゆか先生」のことを理解しながら、たくさんサポートをしてくださった秦野由衣さんには本当に感謝しています。

そしてなにより、この本を手に取ってくださったみなさま、「日本語の森」で日本語を勉強してくださっているみなさま、本当にありがとうございます。みんなからいつも「ありがとう」というメッセージをたくさんもらっているけど、本当に感謝するべきなのは私の方です。

みんな本当にいつもありがとう！ 大好きだよ！

Did you have fun, everybody?

I made this book by using the things I'd felt through direct experience with Japanese language learners, comments on our YouTube channel and social media, and the messages and questions that you all always send in as a reference. When I had just become a Japanese teacher, I had no idea what aspects of Japanese everyone thought were difficult. But when I went live on YouTube, I was able to see everyone's reactions directly, and thanks to the many comments and messages (both good and bad!) I think I got a little bit closer to becoming a better teacher. I believe I was also blessed with the opportunity to write this book thanks to all of you who have helped me grow as a Japanese language teacher.

I am truly grateful to everyone at ASK Publishing for giving me such a wonderful opportunity, and to Yui Hatano for all of her support and understanding of 'Nihongo no Mori' and 'Yuka-sensei.'

And above all, thank you very much to all of you who picked up this book and to everyone studying Japanese at 'Nihongo no Mori.' I always receive lots of thank you messages from everyone, but I'm the one who should really be grateful.

Thank you so much, everyone! I love you!

● **日本語の森株式会社**

「日本語教育を通して世界に貢献する」という理念で、世界中の日本語学習者を対象に日本語学習サービスを提供

【 主なサービス 】
YouTube「日本語の森」、ネット講義サイト／アプリ「nihongonomori.com」
書籍「JLPT N1 この一冊で合格する」「JLPT N2 この一冊で合格する」「JLPT N3 この一冊で合格する」

著者
ちょしゃ
村上由佳
むらかみ ゆか

日本語の森の「ゆか先生」です。
世界中の日本語学習者向けに、
オンライン上で日本語の授業を行っています。

教えて！ゆか先生 日本語会話表現60
おし　　　　　せんせい　　にほんごかいわひょうげん

2021年12月20日　初版第1刷発行
2025年11月5日　初版第3刷発行

著者	村上由佳
DTP／装丁・本文デザイン	株式会社プランテーション（原田裕一、田中楓）
イラスト	伊藤大輔
翻訳	株式会社アミット
印刷・製本	日経印刷株式会社
編集	秦野由衣
発行人	天谷修身
発行	株式会社アスク
	〒162-8558　東京都新宿区下宮比町2-6

乱丁、落丁本はお取り替えいたします。許可なしに転載、複製することを禁じます。
©2021 Yuka Murakami
Printed in Japan　ISBN 978-4-86639-453-4

● 書籍に関するお問い合わせ
https://ask-books.com/support/